MUSICIANS INSTITUTE

PRIVATE LESSON

POWER PLUCKING

A ROCKER'S GUIDE TO ACOUSTIC FINGERSTYLE

BY DALE TURNER

ISBN 978-1-4234-2015-6

HAL•LEONARD®
CORPORATION

7777 W. BLUEMOUND RD. P.O. BOX 13819 MILWAUKEE, WI 53213

In Australia Contact:
Hal Leonard Australia Pty. Ltd.
4 Lentara Court
Cheltenham, Victoria, 3192 Australia
Email: ausadmin@halleonard.com.au

Visit Hal Leonard Online at
www.halleonard.com

Contents

Introduction

Welcome to *Power Plucking—A Rocker's Guide to Acoustic Fingerstyle Guitar*. With this book's 100-plus musical examples (recorded onto 99 CD tracks!), we'll cover all of the essential fingerstyle moves used in rock, from classic to contemporary, and everything in between. We'll also cover some exotic extras, the tools you need to pluck up a storm onstage as an ensemble member, soloist, accompanist, or in your own recordings. Rest assured, if you're a fan of classic pluckers like James Taylor, Paul Simon, Joni Mitchell, John Lennon, Jimmy Page, Eric Clapton, Lindsey Buckingham, or Nick Drake; contemporary singer/songwriters such as John Frusciante, John Mayer, Beck, Jeff Buckley, Elliott Smith, Ani DiFranco, Sarah McLachlan, Shawn Colvin, or Eva Cassidy; or eclectic chops-monsters known on occasion to bust out ferocious fingerstyle moves (e.g., Zakk Wylde, Nuno Bettencourt, Steve Morse, and Eric Johnson), you'll find plenty of material to empower your particular plucking style.

In a nutshell, sounding "right" in rock is a combination of three elements: *plucking-hand technique*, *chord voicings*, and what you do with those voicings as *chords change* (voice leading, common tones, etc.). You won't find these sounds, nor learn how to use them, in a typical classical-guitar method. In fact, in this book, you will find no "classical" arpeggiation sounds. No "classical" counterpoint moves. No "classical" progressions. You'll also find no examples of fingerstyle jazz, blues, new age, or pure country in these pages—just a vast array of ways to take a single chord, redesign it so that it sounds hip, and go nuts—fingerstyle. In other words, make it indisputably rockin'!

All the examples in this book are designed for a *steel-string acoustic* (the only way to rock), played in standard tuning. Many passages are based on variations of a C–G–Ami–F progression. This way, you'll gain a deeper understanding of how to manipulate notes within a familiar chord, and learn how different techniques affect similarly structured changes (i.e., make it easy to hear the different approaches at work between examples.) As the book unfolds, however, numerous other chord sequences will be used. Each chapter is also peppered with tips for you to try out in your own songwriting and cites numerous real-life song/artist examples that feature the techniques being covered.

Although these chapters are presented in an order to incrementally build skill and acquire knowledge, it's understood that some readers might bypass the written text altogether, listen to the accompanying audio tracks, and then flip to the appropriate page to pluck through the transcription. If this sounds like you, just be aware that, because there are so many different examples (well over 100), the audio for some figures might be a few seconds into a particular track. For example, Fig. 1F is located a few seconds into Track 1 of the CD; Fig. 86B is a few seconds into Track 86; etc.

Lastly, realize that there's truly no substitute for studying—up close—the hand movements of technically advanced pluckers. The next time you're watching your guitar teacher play fingerstyle, that underground legend at your local club, or a whiz on an instructional video, study their hand movements intently. You may even consider practicing in front of a mirror, trying to cop their hand positions. Also, don't be afraid to look to fingerstylists in other genres—jazz-based "motherpluckers" like Tuck Andress, Charlie Hunter, Ted Greene, Lenny Breau, or Ralph Towner; wizards of improvised acoustic arrangements like Tommy Emmanuel or Chet Atkins; and classical fingerstylists like Andrew York. These virtuosic pluckers all command a wealth of techniques and approaches adaptable to rock/pop acoustic styles. Sound good? Let the plucking begin!

The Recording

All of the examples on this book's accompanying CD were recorded with two Rode NT-2 mics (blended with a direct signal) through a Presonus BlueTube (stereo mic pre) and HHb Radius 40 Tube Voice Processor (mic pre), direct to hard disk (PowerMAC G4) using Mark of the Unicorn's 1224 (converter) with Digital Performer software. Oh, and a Martin 0001R Auditorium Series, strung with John Pearse strings, was used throughout.

Acknowledgments

This book would not be possible without support from the following, to whom I now offer heaps of thanks: Jeff Schroedl, Chad Johnson, and everybody at Hal Leonard Corporation; GIT Department Head Beth Marlis and all my fellow instructors and students at Musician's Institute; the entire editorial staff at *Guitar One* magazine (Mike Mueller, Chris O'Byrne, Adam Perlmutter, Tom Kolb, and the rest of the lads); and my closest picking compadres (Joy Basu, Darwin DeVitis, Mike Elsner, Bill LaFleur, Roy Marx, Moni Scaria, Ken Snyder, Kevin Tiernan, Chet Urata, and Jeff Young). Of course, my warmest of thanks is reserved for my wife, Hiroko, for her never-ending encouragement, love, and collaborative spirit in all of life's areas. Thank you!

About the Author

Dale Turner teaches guitar, music theory, ear training, sight-reading, and guitar/vocal accompaniment at Hollywood's Musicians Institute. An author of numerous guitar instructional books for Hal Leonard Corporation and Cherry Lane Music, Dale has also transcribed dozens of note-for-note album folios for most of the nation's major publishers. Formerly the West Coast Editor of *Guitar One* magazine, he contributed everything from interview features and instructional pieces (including performing and recording the instructional audio for each issue's CD-ROM) to performance notes and song transcriptions. His written work has also appeared in *Guitar World*, *Guitar Player*, and *Guitar Techniques*, among numerous others.

A former member of David Pritchard's Acoustic Guitar Quartet (featured on *Unassigned Territory*, Zebra/WEA), Dale has also performed with an array of renowned players, including Billy Cobham (Mahavishnu Orchestra, Miles Davis), Larry Klein (Joni Mitchell, Shawn Colvin), Academy Award nominee Bird York, Eric "Bobo" Correa (Cypress Hill), and Josh Levy (Big Bad Voodoo Daddy).

Under his own name, Dale Turner has issued two full-length albums. The first, *Interpretations*, is an intimate recording of solo arrangements for acoustic guitar and voice, featuring Queen's "Bohemian Rhapsody," the Beach Boys' "God Only Knows," Jimi Hendrix's "Castles Made of Sand," and other 1960s-'70s classics. His latest release, *On the Outskirts of the In-Crowd*, is an album of original compositions, featuring Turner performing all of the instruments—vocals, guitar, bass, drums, piano, accordion, and mandolin.

In 1991, Turner received his bachelor's degree in Studio/Jazz Guitar Performance from the University of Southern California, where he studied with E.C. "Duke" Miller, Steve Watson, Paul LaRose, Joe Diorio, Richard Smith, and Andrew York. He later went on to teach at USC as a part-time pop/rock guitar instructor/lecturer (1993–95). For more information, feel free to visit Turner at his own site on the World Wide Web, www.intimateaudio.com.

Fingerstyle Basics

1

We'll open this book with some plucking fundamentals, addressing finger assignments, hand position, and nail care. Photos are also included, which you can use as a "model" for your own hand's placement. If you feel strain or discomfort in your plucking hand while practicing certain passages in this book, refer back to these pages to fine-tune your technique. This section also details the symbols unique to finger-style and the different notation approaches used.

Finger Assignments: Plucking- and Fretting-Hand Symbols

The "plucking" approach used by beginning fingerstylists is often random—arbitrary finger moves that provide no foundation for learning and developing a command over trickier moves. If this sounds like you, do yourself a favor and get grounded in "proper" fingerstyle technique first: using a specific combination of plucking-hand fingers to sound certain strings.

As a default plucking approach, accomplished fingerstylists use their thumb to play strings 4–6, and their remaining digits—index, middle, and ring fingers—to pluck the third (G), second (B), and first (E) strings, respectively. With that said, as this book progresses, you *will* encounter examples where this "rule" is broken. Hence, between the notation and tab staves of each figure, fingers will be specified using the standardized symbols from classical guitar: *p*=thumb, *i*=index, *m*=middle, and *a*=ring. These symbols are abbreviations for the Spanish names for fingers—*p* ("pulgar," or "thumb"), *i* ("indice," or "index"), *m* ("medio," or "middle"), and *a* ("anular," or "ring")—because much of early classical-guitar repertoire, where fingerstyle notation first became codified, stems from Spanish guitar literature. In general, though, it's safe to approach plucking as follows: thumb (*p*) for strings 4–6, and index (*i*), middle (*m*), and ring (*a*) fingers for the third, second, and first strings, respectively.

In many cases, fret-hand fingering suggestions are included as well. Fret-hand fingers are represented in numerical fashion (*1*=index, *2*=middle, *3*=ring, *4*=pinky), while the thumb is specified with a "T." I strongly recommended that you get accustomed to using your fret-hand's thumb to fret many of the bass notes found in this book. In every case it is suggested, the thumb will free up other fingers to cleanly fret, or sustain, notes used as common tones between changing chords, or other tricky moves. Fret-hand fingers will be written next to noteheads, if clarification is needed.

Plucking-Hand Fingers

Fretting-Hand Fingers

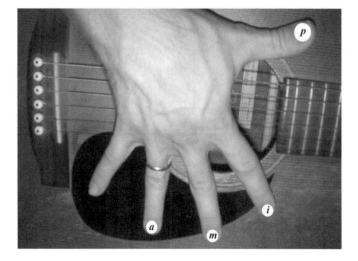

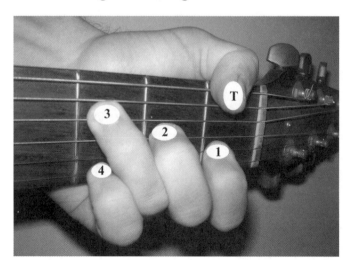

The Plucking-Hand's Position

To eliminate tension in your plucking-hand fingers and avoid straining (something you may notice early on in some of our quicker arpeggio figures), position your hand as follows until you're instructed otherwise: With your plucking-hand's wrist cocked at a slight angle, place the outside edge of your thumb (*p*) along any of the lower strings (strings 4–6). Point the thumb slightly towards the neck, so it doesn't have to pluck on the same physical plane as other fingers—you don't want your thumb to collide with other digits when you pluck. Then, with your fingers arched like a crescent, do the same with your index (*i*), middle (*m*), and ring (*a*) fingers on strings 3–1, respectively, contacting the strings at a slight angle, where flesh and nail meet. This is a preparation posture referred to as *planting*. (Notice how close together—yet relaxed—the fingers are in the photo below.) For maximum power and (eventual) control, move your thumb at its *first knuckle only*—the point where it joins the hand—to pluck strings 4–6. For your index (*i*), middle (*m*), and ring (*a*) fingers, pluck their assigned strings using a motion similar to squeezing a trigger (i.e., pushing your fingertips through the strings, not "pulling" on them), bending your digits from the *first knuckle only*. To keep notes ringing together as much as possible, *after* your fingers engage in their respective plucking motions, they should end up in a free-floating position, away from the strings. This is referred to as *free stroke*.

Fingers Arched Like a "Crescent"

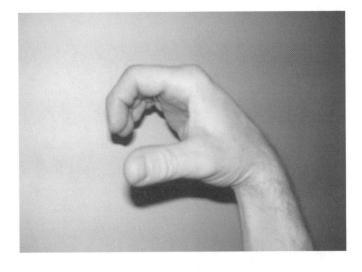

"Trigger-Pulling" Motion

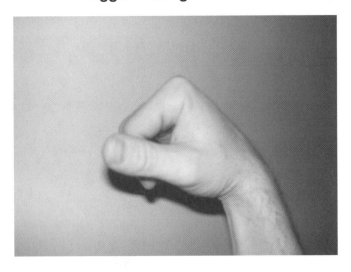

Proper "Planting" Position (Good!)

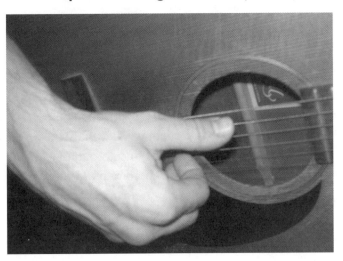

Improper Position with Hand Strain (Bad!)

A Note on Nail Care

For acoustic plucking, having a little extra length in your fingernails helps; using them in conjunction with your fingertips' flesh produces a warm, projecting tone. Fingernails also control dynamics better than flesh alone and provide more variations in tone color. (Using only your fingertip pads as a string's point of contact is fine; however, be wary of developing slight points of irritation, and possibly small blisters, if you're plucking for the first time. Remember how sore your fret-hand's fingertips were the first time you fretted notes on your guitar?) If you stop biting your nails long enough to start getting some length out of them, consider grooming them with a high-quality nail file; shape each nail into an oval, each nail extending approximately 1–2 millimeters past your finger's tip. After shaping the nail with the file's rougher edge, smooth over the rough spots with the file's "fine" side, or very fine sandpaper (500-plus grade). In playing the forthcoming musical examples, your ability to perform specific finger moves will dictate when you need to fine-tune nail length (i.e., if you can't "push" your fingers through the strings in the manner described in the previous section because your nails are "catching" the string, file them shorter). Once your nails are properly shaped, you might even apply clear nail polish to them for added strength. That way, your nails won't get shredded when you're plucking on steel strings. (Note: If you already play a nylon-string or classical guitar using your longer nails and wish to preserve them, try angling your fingers slightly so that *only* your fingertip pads touch the strings.)

Freshly Filed Fingernails

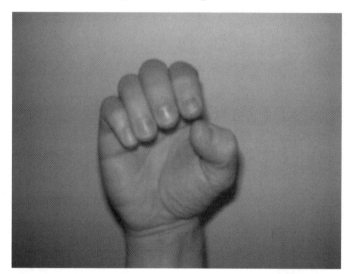

Notational Style

Before we launch into our introductory figures, you'll want to understand some notation styles used in fingerstyle guitar. For instance, many passages in this book are written *divisi* style—using opposing stems to clarify independent voices (melody and bass) on a single staff. In other instances, passages are notated in standard fashion—a single "part" written on the staff. In virtually every case, you'll want notes to ring together as much as possible. (As a reminder, you'll often see the phrase "let ring throughout" included between notation and tab staves.) A good rule of thumb to follow: For every chord name written overhead (that figure's harmonic analysis), keep your fingers fretted until the name of the next, new chord appears overhead.

Piano-Style Plucking

2

To get you up and running with some usable moves, let's examine the relatively simple plucking-hand combinations that are used in *piano-style* accompaniment parts. If you're wondering how on earth "piano-style" plucking translates to rocking, consider this fact: If you're a serious guitarist, bent on becoming as diverse as possible, it's only a matter of time before you try to arrange a piano-based pop/rock hit for guitar—perhaps to accompany your own vocal, someone else in a duo setting, or to simply cop that song's piano intro. Not sold yet? A short list of well-known classic-to-modern rock acts that occasionally prefer a piano-centric sound include the Beatles ("Let It Be"), Beach Boys ("God Only Knows"), John Lennon ("Imagine"), the Eagles ("Desperado"), Queen ("Bohemian Rhapsody"), Allman Brothers ("Ramblin' Man")—even Van Halen ("Jump") and Mötley Crüe ("Home Sweet Home")! Meanwhile, there are tons of rock/pop acts whose sound stems entirely from piano: Elton John, Billy Joel, Carole King, Bruce Hornsby, Tori Amos, Fiona Apple, Norah Jones, Ben Folds, and so on. Of course, acoustic ballads and mellower rock/pop offerings like Eric Clapton's "Tears in Heaven," and much of Eva Cassidy's acoustic accompaniment, are entirely rooted in this "pianistic" guitar sound. And we can't leave out the piano-inspired electric-guitar riffs in songs by bands like Aerosmith ("Dream On") and No Doubt ("Don't Speak"), among others.

Clearly, plucking "piano style" is a foundational sound—a universal approach, usable in most forms of rock. But if you want to play these songs on acoustic, or create accompaniment parts similar to them in your own songs, it helps to *think* like a pianist. That all begins with developing a deeper understanding of triads and 7th chords (and their inversions), and how pianists voice them—the "spread" between notes in bass and upper registers. But don't worry—a lot of this can be accomplished by revamping familiar shapes.

Dissecting the Fundamental Plucking Pattern

Figs. 1A–H take four common open chords—C (C–E–G), G (G–B–D), Ami (A–C–E), and F (F–A–C)—and extract from them (note exact fingerings, as well as which notes are omitted) all the elements of a basic "pianistic" plucking approach, building up to Fig. 1H. The aim here is to make it easier to understand its individual components, and hone in on (i.e., practice) specific plucking/fretting motions. For instance, think of Fig. 1B as the sustained bass notes of a pianist's left hand, with three-note chords voiced above with the right hand (Fig. 1C). From there, it can be broken down as follows: On beats 1 and 3, each triad's top notes are plucked with the index (*i*) and middle (*m*) fingers, while the thumb (*p*) simultaneously plucks bass notes (Fig. 1D). Then practice plucking strings 2–3 in quarter notes against the half-note bass (Fig. 1E). Once you're comfortable with that, try squeezing in an extra thumb stroke between the cracks of the attacks (on the "and" of each beat) on strings 2–3 (Fig. 1F). Then combine all of the thumb's moves and focus on it solely (Fig. 1G). Overall, your plucking hand is repeating a physical pattern that is two beats in length. Put it all together (Fig. 1H) and you're ready to start using this plucking approach to play through all sorts of other progressions, with more interesting voicings. (Note: Using "thumb fretting" for the F chord in this passage makes it possible to keep the upper notes of Am ringing as you transition to F. This isn't possible with an F barre-chord approach.)

Track 1

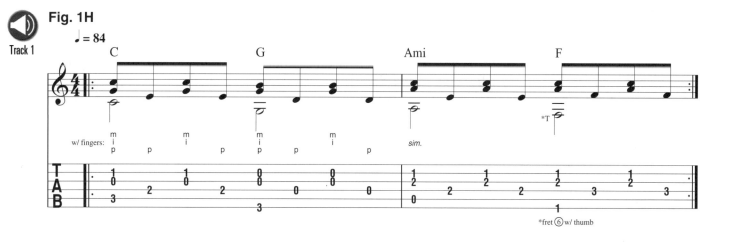

Barre Chord "Piano-Style" Workout

Figs. 2A–B apply the previous, new piano-style approach to fully fretted shapes; again, the plucking-hand thumb (*p*) plays strings 4–6, while your index (*i*) and middle (*m*) fingers are assigned to strings 2–3. Note that all of the three-note chord fingerings in this section (and other triad moves throughout this book) are not chosen for *ease* of playability; they are chosen to achieve smooth *voice leading*—maintaining common tones between chords, or moving each note within a chord a minimal distance to form the next chord. This is a key ingredient in any effective "background" part, as it keeps an accompaniment passage's notes confined to a small harmonic range (think of it as sounding "horizontal," as opposed to "vertical"), so as to not conflict with the vocals or other melody instrument.

Track 2

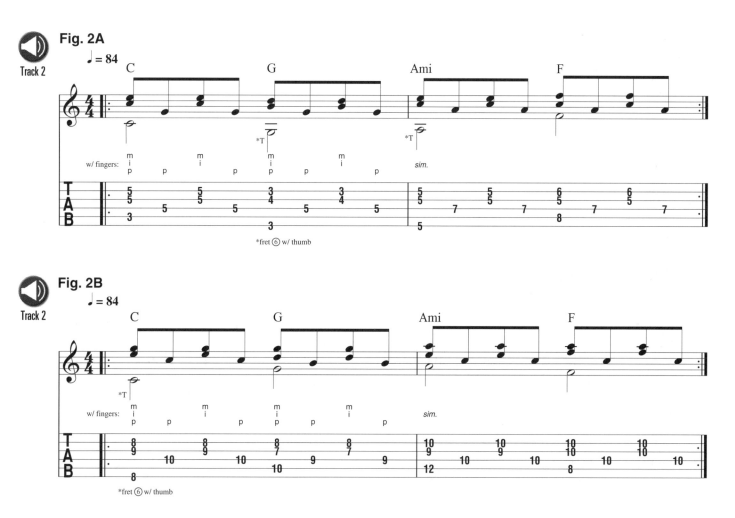

Breaking the Rules!

To create further separation between bass notes and upper-register triads, **Figs. 3A–B** shift the plucking hand's fingers to higher strings, while maintaining the same "thumbed bass notes" approach (strings 5–6), only now using *i* and *m* fingers to pluck strings 2–1, respectively. (The thumb also has to cross over to pluck string 3.) Basically, we're now able to create a "wider-sounding" accompaniment texture using the exact same plucking-hand approach. This will be the first of many times we break the "finger assignments" rule discussed in this book's opening chapter. Rock is all about rebellion!

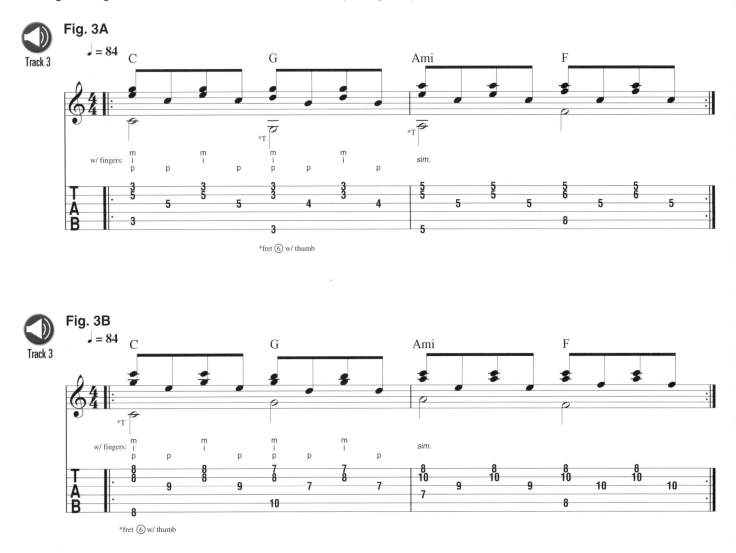

Syncopated Bass Notes

The choruses of Eric Clapton's "Tears in Heaven" toy with triads on higher strings much like this chapter's earlier figures, only Clapton plucks chords similar to those in **Figs. 4A–B**. The key difference here is, the index (*i*), middle (*m*), and ring (*a*) fingers simultaneously pluck each chord's highest strings while the thumb plays a syncopated eighth-note rhythm. (Interestingly, this "thumb" rhythm is identical to that of Fig. 1G, only here it's applied to the same note throughout.) Meanwhile, Fig. 4B presents the first embellishment of our C–G–Ami–F progression; selected tones are added, keeping a G common tone on top, which creates fancier chord names like Am7 (A–C–E–G) and Fadd2 (F–A–C–G), the latter of which requires thumb-fretting. In general, this type of upper-register common-tone approach is key to making otherwise ordinary voicings "sparkle" in acoustic rock. Keep your eyes and ears peeled for more!

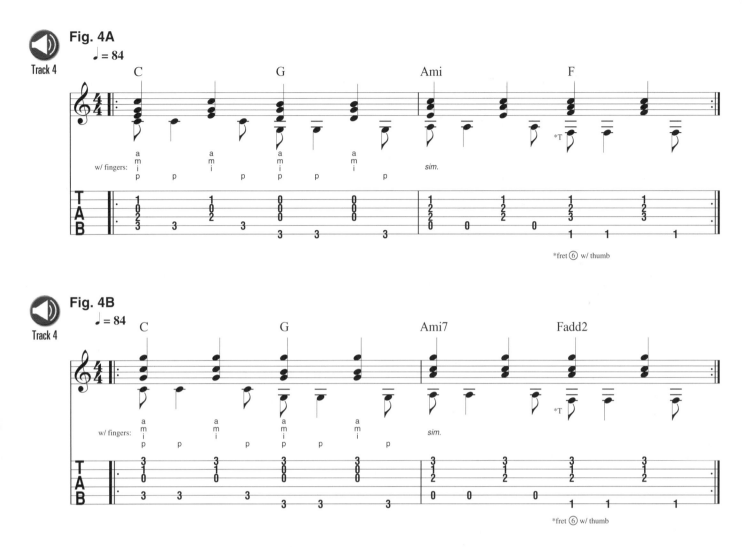

Fig. 4A
Track 4

Fig. 4B
Track 4

*fret ⑥ w/ thumb

Melodic Motifs: 4/4 Meter

Fig. 5 stretches out the previous two-beat pattern to fill a full 4/4 measure (four beats). Lurking within this figure is a tasty *melodic motif*—a repeated melodic idea or "theme"—that alternates between C (fret 1) and B (open) on the second string. This type of compositional approach—interjecting a melodic focal point—is commonly used to create "rock-sounding" fingerstyle passages. Of course, this process wreaks havoc on chord names—in this case, producing Cma7 (C–E–G–B), Gsus4 (G–C–D), and Emi/A (A–E–G–B), among others. But everything's still rooted in our basic C–G–Ami–F progression. We'll get deeper into the science behind tweaking basic chords in Chapter 6 ("Open-Chord Ornaments"), Chapter 7 ("Pedal Point and Inversion"), and Chapter 11 ("Open-Chord Extras").

Fig. 5
Track 5

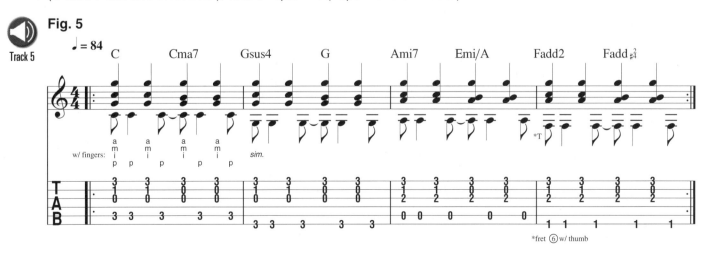

*fret ⑥ w/ thumb

Melodic Motifs: 3/4 Meter

Not all forms of rock fall under the umbrella of 4/4 meter, of course. For this reason, you'll want to get comfortable plucking through other time signatures, like 3/4. **Fig. 6** is a three-beat adaptation of our earlier "Tears in Heaven" plucking style. This passage contains variations on G, Emi, C, and Ami chords, in homage to singer/songwriter (and stellar self-accompanist) Jeff Buckley, and loosely based on his song "Eternal Life." Note the descending G–F♯–E motif on string 1, which is used atop every passing chord.

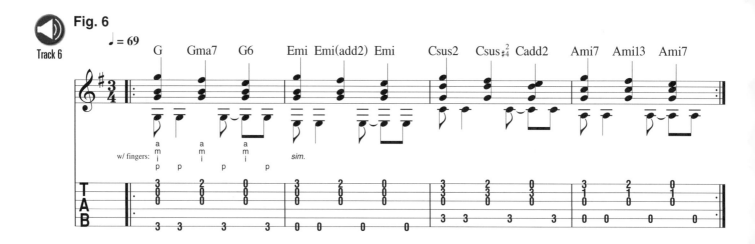

Piano-Style Plucking with Stepwise Bass line

Fig. 7 plugs earlier plucking-hand approaches into a new handful of voicings, which, like Figs. 1–5, are all in the key of C and feature upper-register common tones. The new element here is the use of *inversions*—like Gadd2/B—to create a stepwise C–B–A bass line between C5 and Ami7. This stepwise movement continues throughout the riff, rewarding us with a figure that features a G common tone (third fret, first string) atop chords built from every note in the C scale. (Inversions and related sounds are explored in detail in Chapter 7.)

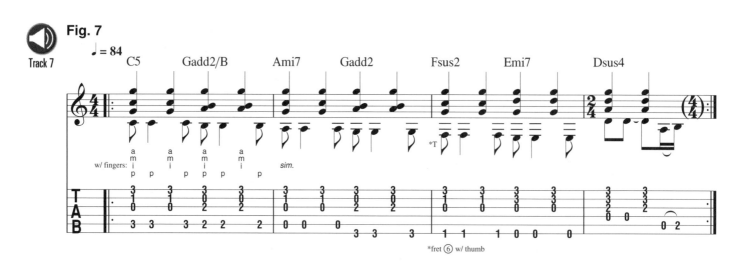

Music Box Dancer

Figs. 8A–B depict a touch of *arpeggiation*—plucking one note at a time, within a sustained chord shape—added to piano-like accompaniment. (Arpeggio moves are studied in-depth in the next chapter.) In Fig. 8A, the upper notes, plucked with a repeating *a–m–i–m* pattern, become the focal point, while the thumb plucks a quarter-note bass. In Fig. 8B, the roles reverse: The bass line, an arpeggiation in steady eighth notes from the thumb on strings 5–3, is now central, while an *m–i* move sounds quarter notes on strings 2–1. Some of you "pluckers" may find this pair of examples to be the trickiest so far, as each beat features different combinations of the *i*, *m*, and *a* fingers played simultaneously with thumbed notes. The end result is a fairly "pretty" sound, though, not unlike that of a music box, especially when played in higher registers (with a capo, for instance).

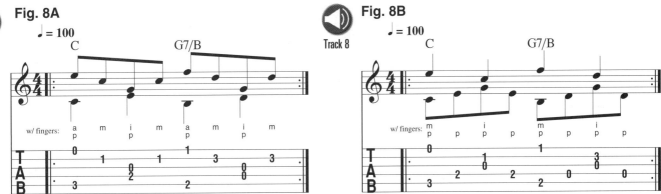

Milking the *"m–i"* Combination

Figs. 9A–B also break our basic plucking rules, using the *m–i* finger combination to pluck notes on strings 2–1 *and* 3–2. Both figures feature the same thumb-plucking pattern; the only thing that changes from one figure to the next is the order in which the highest string pair is plucked.

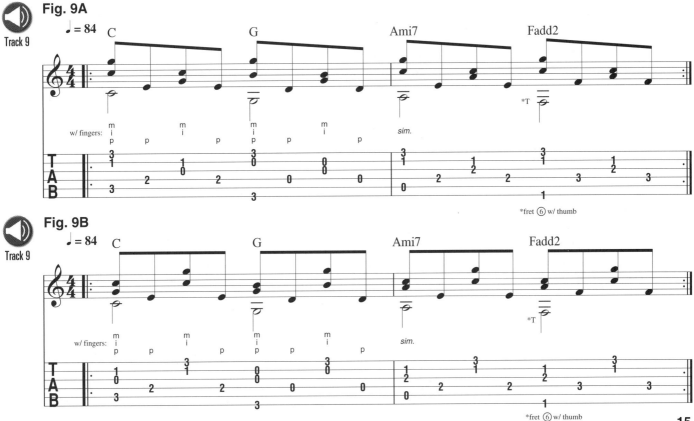

Fig. 10A continues to "milk" the *i–m* plucking movements, only this time the combination is played over eighth-note arpeggiation from the thumb. Also, a *double stop* (two-note chord partial) containing the notes C and G is emphasized within every chord, functioning as a "hook," or repetitive element, that is also present in **Fig. 10B**.

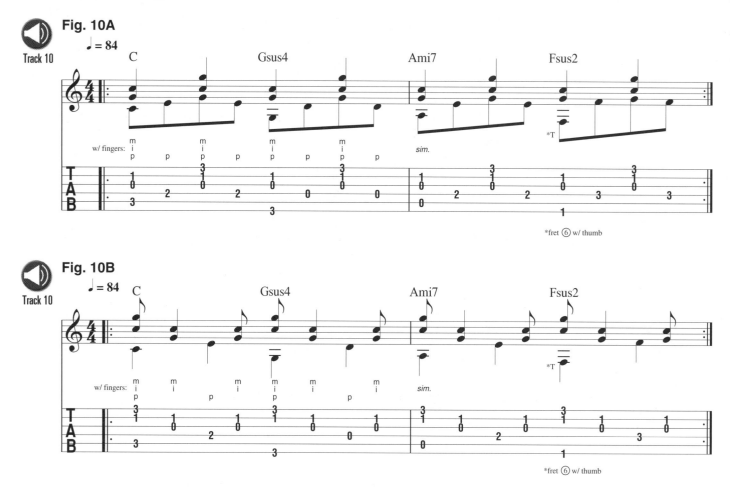

Adding Seventh Chords to the Mix

If you tackle classic-rock songs from any of the bands listed at this chapter's outset, it's a given that you'll find yourself plucking some seventh-chord moves. Towards that end, **Fig. 11A** turns a standard C–Ami–Dmi–G progression into Cma7–Ami7–Dmi7–G7 changes, replete with *suspended* voicings (A7sus4, D7sus4, and G7sus4) that generate melodic movement with the voices of each chord. Essentially, we're replacing the 3rd of each chord (C, in Ami7) with a 4th (D, in Ami7), creating an unresolved effect (A7sus4). **Fig. 11B** behaves similarly, only with a more Beatles-esque Cma7–A7–D7–G7 change.

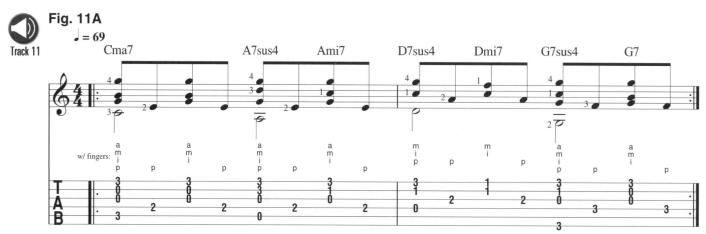

Fig. 11B

Track 11

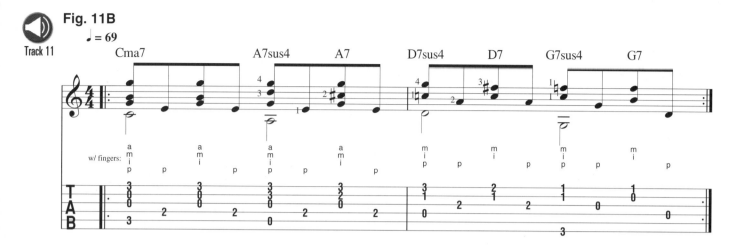

This chapter's final example, **Fig. 12**, combines some fairly uncommon "open" versions of dominant-seventh chords (F#7, B7, etc.) with even less-common suspended voicings (F#7sus4, B7sus4, etc.). Here, you'll find ample "rule-breaking," as various string pairs that are normally off-limits to all but the thumb are plucked together with the thumb (*p*) and index finger (*i*).

Fig. 12

Track 12

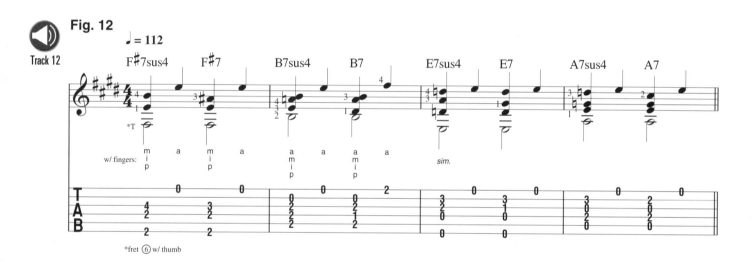

*fret ⑥ w/ thumb

Congratulations! You've just run your plucking hands through an assortment of tricky piano-style moves and, in the process, learned a bunch of new chord voicings. Add more arpeggiation to the mix, and you'll be armed with a wealth of "pianistic/guitaristic" sounds. That's where this book's next chapter comes in.

3 Arpeggiated Accompaniment

As we encountered for a brief moment back in Chapter 2, the plucking-hand's fingers can also be used one at a time to create *arpeggios*—essentially a "broken chord" whose notes are played one after another rather than all at once. In this section, we'll go gonzo on assorted arpeggio moves, looking at figures with different plucking-hand finger combinations, wider note spacing, trickier rhythms, and varying tempos, as made famous by pluckers ranging from Bob Dylan, Paul Simon, James Taylor, and John Lennon to Jimmy Page, Lindsey Buckingham, and Alex Lifeson—as well as more contemporary artists like Sheryl Crow, Jeff Buckley, and Elliott Smith.

Ascending "Ripple" Effect

In **Fig. 13A**, the pick hand arpeggiates eighth notes in an ascending *p–p–i–m* pattern, reminiscent of James Taylor's work in "Shower the People." Remember to keep your fingers relaxed and close—but not squeezed—together to minimize hand strain as you pluck individual strings. There should be *zero* tension in your plucking hand as you play through every example in this book. (Look back at the hand-position photos in Chapter 1 for examples.) At the same time, make every effort to keep your fingertips as close to the strings as possible; that will make it easier to play faster figures.

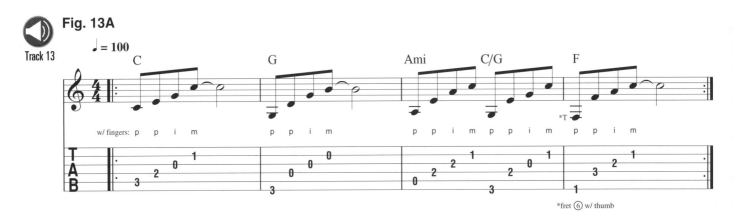

Fig. 13A
Track 13

Fig. 13B is a variation of the previous example, this time with each chord's arpeggiation punctuated with a double stop (two notes plucked simultaneously with the *m–a* fingers) or triple stop (three notes plucked simultaneously with the *i–m–a* fingers), and some more thumb activity. The simple act of adding two- and three-note sounds atop arpeggiated chords instantly makes figures feel more "rock" oriented.

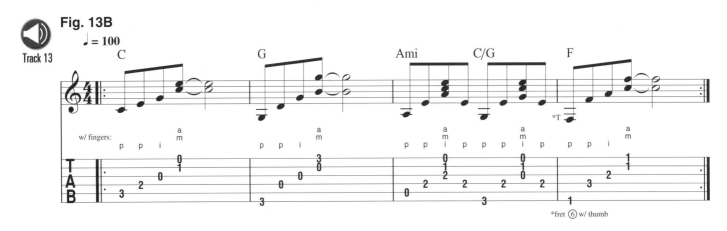

Fig. 13B
Track 13

Latin-Rock Arpeggiated Rhythms

Fig. 14 contains some Latin rock–tinged arpeggios—the "Latin" aspect stemming from the specific blend of eighth and sixteenth notes. Note that the plucking-hand's thumb has to be quickly repositioned as it grapples with notes on strings 4–6.

Fig. 14

Track 14

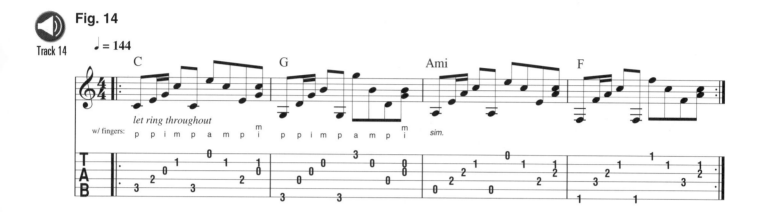

Fig. 15 maintains our quasi Latin-rock vibe, this time using fully fretted chord shapes, the G and F forms punctuated with double stops on strings 2–3. Again, note the "rule-breaking"—our default finger-style approach is modified so that our *i–m–a* fingers pluck strings 4–2, respectively, during the quick arpeggiations of C and Ami chords.

Fig. 15

Track 15

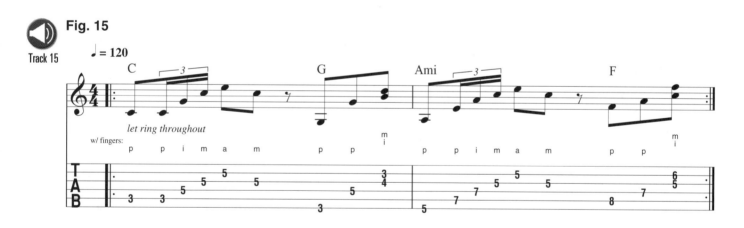

Infectious 3/4 Figure

Sheryl Crow fans, particularly those enamored with her hit "Strong Enough," will surely dig the "pluck-ings" of **Fig. 16**—a similar progression, but spiced up with trickier arpeggios and *accented* chord partials on the "and" of beat 3. Pluck slightly louder at these points, where you see the ">" (accent) symbol. Resist the temptation to "pull" on the strings to get a louder sound; just use more "trigger pulling" power—quicker motions, coupled with more intensity.

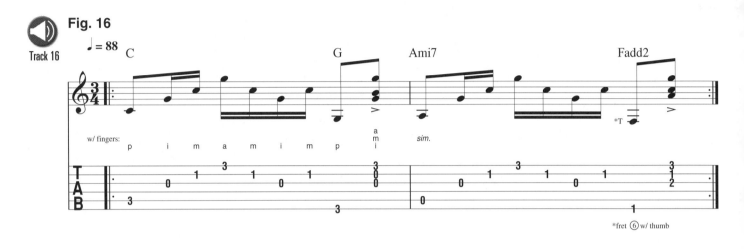

Arpeggios with "Gap Spacing"

The next handful of figures involve plucking strings found at wider distances apart—still ascending moves, but with a string skip in the middle, as in **Fig. 17**, which is modeled loosely after Led Zeppelin's "Babe, I'm Gonna Leave You." In this riff, use a *p–p–i* plucking pattern (no *m* finger) to sound the lowest strings, reserving the *a* finger for the G (fret 3) and E (open) notes on the first string. Essentially, this all boils down to a *p–i–a* finger combination, a tricky maneuver we'll be chipping away at for a while.

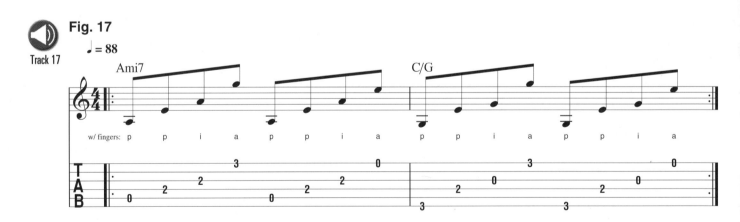

Buckingham's Plucking Span

Fig. 18A's "gap spacing" arpeggio moves—again, plucked with the *p–i–a* fingers—are a nod to Lindsey Buckingham's plucking in Fleetwood Mac's "Bleed to Love Her." Notice that each chord features our familiar G (third fret, first string) common tone in the highest register, and that beats 1–3 of each bar have a "two-against-three" feel—the same three-note arpeggio pattern stated twice over the span of three beats. This rhythmic effect is referred to as *hemiola*, and will be revisited in later examples.

Fig. 18A

Track 18

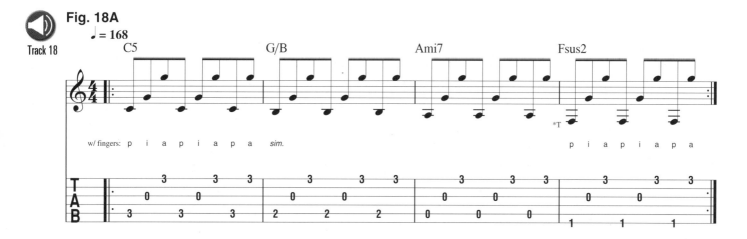

Fig. 18B illustrates a "tightened up" version of the previous passage, with the *i–m* fingers assigned to strings 2–1, respectively (another rule breaker!). Here, the note C (first fret, second string) is added and maintained throughout each voicing, creating a motif as it interacts with the high G note in each chord.

Fig. 18B

Track 18

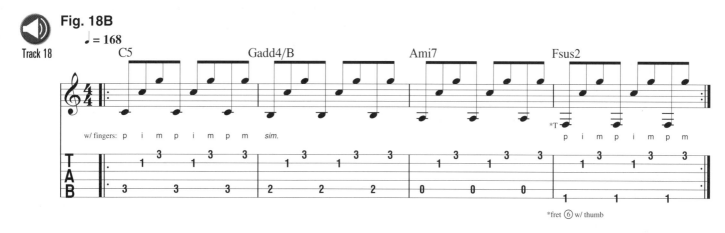

*fret ⑥ w/ thumb

Mojo Workin'

This last "gap spacing" example [**Fig. 19**] requires a rapid-fire *p–i–m–i–a* plucking combination, similar to what Jeff Buckley used in "Mojo Pin." The "gap" portion occurs between the *i* and *a* fingers, which are used to quickly pluck the third and first strings, respectively. Try not to rush or slow down during the arpeggiated portions, allowing the highest note (beats 2 and 4) to be consistently sustained for an entire beat.

Fig. 19

Track 19

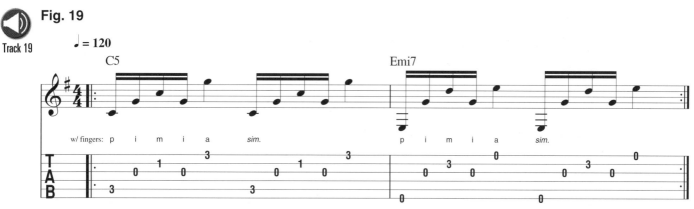

Metronomic Madness

To tame tricky passages like the previous example or to simply improve your time feel, consider practicing along with a *metronome*, a device that emits a steady, unerring pulse, adjustable to a variety of speeds that are measured in *beats per minute* (bpm). For instance, if you can't comfortably roll your fingers through a figure's suggested tempo, find a slower setting on your metronome—the fastest tempo at which you can play the figure, with no hand strain, before it falls apart. Once you've established that tempo (the high end of your comfort zone), work up from there by gradually increasing metronome speed until your goal tempo has been reached. This may take days, so be patient! Keep a daily record of your metronome settings so that you can see on paper how much you've improved.

Tricky Triplets

Want trickier arpeggios? *Triplets*, three evenly spaced attacks per beat, present the next level of difficulty. In **Fig. 20**, an ascending *p–i–m* roll, inspired by moves in Elliott Smith's "White Lady," is plugged into our familiar progression. As you play through this figure, try *replanting* your fingers on the strings a millisecond before the repetition of each plucking-hand pattern. Essentially, the exact moment your thumb (*p*) plucks a string, your other fingers (*i–m*) should already be touching their respective strings, prepared to pluck. Obviously, when you play the passage slowly, this "replanting" (a legitimate classical-guitar trick for playing fast arpeggios) will stop the highest strings from ringing for a brief period. But when played at tempo, this break in sound will be imperceptible.

Fig. 20

Track 20

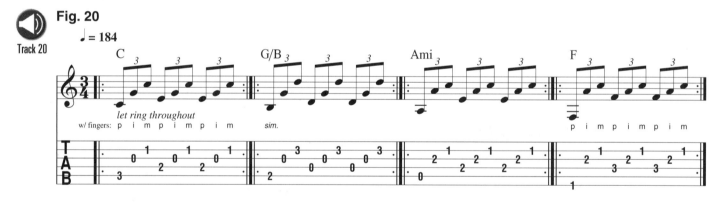

Reverse *p–i–m* Pattern

In many examples, we've used a *p–i–m* finger combination to achieve various effects. With **Fig. 21**, let's use these same fingers to play arpeggios, but change the order in which they're used. Here, a *p–m–i* arrangement is plugged into a modern-sounding sequence of chords.

Fig. 21

Track 21

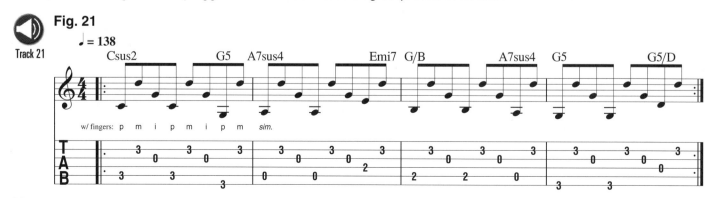

Outside/Inside Plucking

In songs such as Bob Dylan's "Don't Think Twice, It's Alright," Simon and Garfunkel's "The Boxer," and Fleetwood Mac's "Landslide," you'll hear the *p*, *i*, and *m* fingers used to arpeggiate "outer" then "inner" notes of a chord, resulting in a *p–m–p–i* pattern [**Fig. 22**]. This figure marks the first time we've created arpeggio sounds without "rolling" our fingers. For that reason, you may find it difficult to balance the volume of each pluck. To tame your finger moves and balance the arpeggiated texture, try plucking each bass note—the fifth-string notes of C, G/B, and Ami, and the sixth string of F—*slightly* louder (just enough so a listener can detect its pulse) than the higher strings.

Fig. 22

Track 22

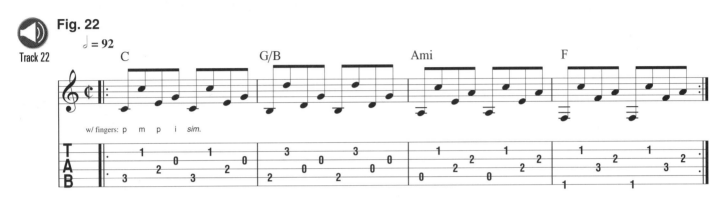

Fig. 23 expands upon our earlier outside/inside plucking passage, adding a common tone, E (open first string), to the upper register of each chord's arpeggio. Again, the fact that this note is reiterated throughout binds each chord with a common thread—that magical "hook" or "motif" that you hear in so many great acoustic rock riffs. Also, notice that this figure relies on *p–i–p–m* plucking, but the *m* finger is shifted to hit the first string (instead of the second)—a slap in the face of hardcore classicists everywhere!

Fig. 23

Track 23

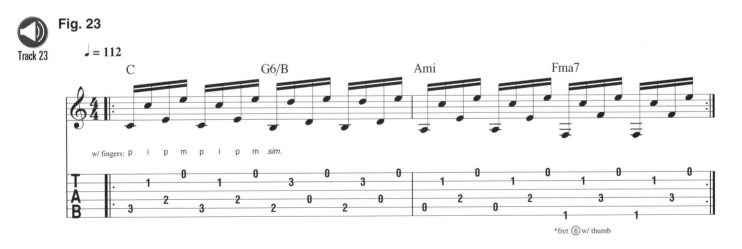

*fret ⑥ w/ thumb

Cracking the Compositional Whip!

Hopefully, some of the figures you encounter in this book will serve as inspiration for plucking-hand approaches or voicings that act as a catalyst for some of your own creations. Beyond this book's varied voicings, don't be afraid to simply place your fret-hand fingers on some uncommon note combinations—like those in **Fig. 24**, for instance—and rip through them with some of your practiced plucking-hand moves for some surprising results. This particular example, due to the fretting of notes near the middle of the neck, played in conjunction with open strings, creates some *stepwise note cascades*—scalar moves similar to those in Fleetwood Mac's "Big Love" and Rush's "Closer to the Heart." Despite all the trickery, this passage still outlines our time-tested C–G–Ami–F progression.

Fig. 24

"Pinch" Patterns with Arpeggiation

So far, all of our arpeggiation techniques have involved plucking one note at a time within individual chords. We've yet to simultaneously pluck a bass note *and* upper-register chord tones, spinning them into arpeggiated mayhem. In **Figs. 25A–B**, the "outer" notes of each chord are plucked—or "pinched"—on the downbeat (beat 1), followed by *p–m–p–i* arpeggiation not unlike our earlier outside/inside plucking moves. Fig. 25A presents the example with basic open chords. Fig. 25B revamps each voicing to include a G common tone on top, morphing the original figure from "square" to "hip."

Fig. 25A

Fig. 25B

Track 25

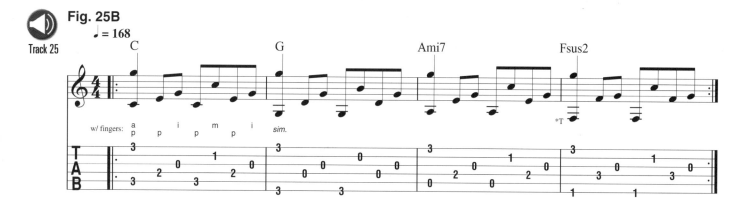

It's worth noting that the *exact* plucking combination in Figs. 25A–B surfaces in countless Beatles songs, from "Dear Prudence" and "Happiness Is a Warm Gun" to "Julia" (all played by John Lennon). You'll also hear it in classic acoustic-rock cuts like Blind Faith's "Can't Find My Way Home," Kansas's "Dust in the Wind," and many more. This combination of arpeggios and bass notes is strikingly similar to a plucking style called *Travis picking*, a country-like accompaniment that was curiously foundational for much of the acoustic-rock plucking of the sixties and seventies. That factual nugget more than merits our devotion to this approach in the next chapter.

But before we delve deep into Travis picking, amp up your arpeggio chops with this tricky passage [**Fig. 26**], a descending cascade of eighth notes (another three-against-four hemiola figure), played against thumb-plucked quarter notes. This one owes a debt to Buckingham's plucking in the choruses of Fleetwood Mac's "Landslide."

Fig. 26

Track 26

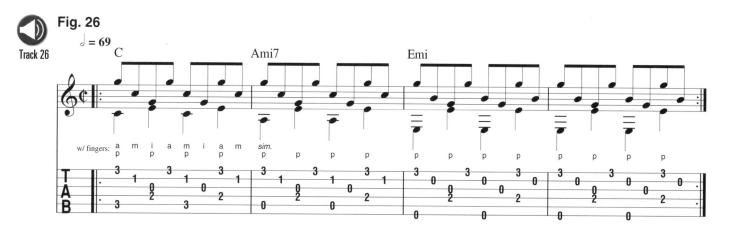

Travis Picking

4

At the heart of acoustic-driven classic-rock cuts like John Lennon's "Julia," Harry Nilsson's "Coconut," John Denver's "Take Me Home (Country Roads)," Dan Fogelberg's "Leader of the Band," and countless others, you'll find *Travis picking*, a fingerstyle technique named after guitar virtuoso Merle Travis. This useful plucking style involves articulating chord-tone (root, 3rd, and 5th) bass notes with the thumb (authentic Travis-pickers use a thumbpick), and higher-string notes with the index, middle, and ring fingers. Though it's rooted in country music (Merle Travis was a country-music session veteran in the 1940s–'50s), Travis picking had an impact and influence on innumerable acoustic-rock guitar greats in the 1960s–'70s; in addition to those cited previously, the list of pluckers includes Nick Drake, Stephen Stills, Lindsey Buckingham, Gordon Lightfoot, Paul Simon, and Jim Croce. Going further back, it also forged much of Scotty Moore's early work with Elvis, including "Baby, Let's Play House" and "Just Because," which were played on electric and helped give birth to rockabilly. More recently, it's a key component to the pluckings of modern singer/songwriters like Elliott Smith.

Although "true" Travis picking applies slight palm mutes to each bass note and, in a country-style ensemble, the bass guitar often doubles these notes, in the interest of making these types of passages sound at home in a rock setting, we'll eliminate muting from the equation. Further, to keep them rooted in rock in your own music, gravitate towards figures in which the alternated bass notes are mostly *above* your chord's root (look back to Figs. 25A–B). Further tips on transforming these passages into more "rockin'" sounds are forthcoming.

Developing Independence Between Melody and Bass

Accomplished Travis-pickers have the ability to—whenever the spirit moves them—pluck any combination of treble strings, using any available *i*, *m*, or *a* finger, without having their thumb-plucked bass part falter. To raise your game to this level, you need to spend time refining the *independence* between these two voices: melody and bass. Using various approaches of a C (C–E–G) chord, this chapter's opening series of exercises does just that.

In **Fig. 27A**, you'll see a C–G (root–5th) alternating bass pattern, with notes sounding on beats 1 and 3. (In Travis picking, root–5th alternating bass lines are most common, but root–3rd combinations do exist. We'll pluck through some of these towards the end of this chapter.) To play this properly, begin by fretting an open-position C chord, whereby your fret-hand's third finger voices the root (C) on the fifth string (third fret). Next, switch this finger back and forth between the fifth and sixth strings, alternating between the C and G (third fret, sixth string) bass notes, plucking each with your thumb. However, *do not* allow these notes to ring together by way of barring, or fretting one of them with your fourth finger. In **Fig. 27B**, our introductory bass pattern is modified into a C–E–G–E line, in which a different chord tone is sounded on each beat. Again, grab each of the notes on the fifth and sixth strings by moving your fret-hand's third finger back and forth; it's okay for the fourth string to ring throughout. All of the examples in the first part of this chapter will be built upon this bass line, so you'd be best served to get this down.

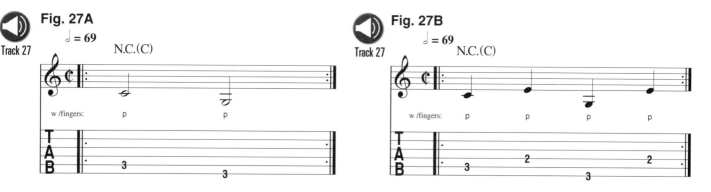

Fig. 27A
Track 27
♩ = 69
N.C.(C)
w /fingers: p p

Fig. 27B
Track 27
♩ = 69
N.C.(C)
w /fingers: p p p p

Adding a Single Melody Note

In **Fig. 28A**, a single note (C) is added to our earlier bass line, plucked on each individual beat (in synch with the bass line) using the *m* finger. Meanwhile, in **Fig. 28B**, our new C note is stated in half notes (i.e., sustained for two beats each). This requires a subtle form of rhythmic independence between your plucked bass notes (the quarter notes) and sustained melody notes (half notes) because all of these notes are not plucked simultaneously, as was the case in the previous example. Basically, you *do not* want your picked bass notes to drown out the pitches on your second string, or, if you're accidentally replanting your plucking fingers, force them to stop ringing. (Note: From here on out, our bass lines will appear as down-stemmed notes and melody notes will be up-stemmed.)

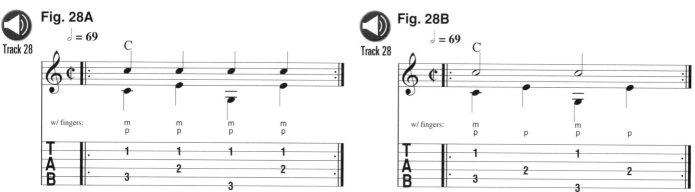

Fig. 28A
Track 28
♩ = 69
C
w/ fingers: m m m m / p p p p

Fig. 28B
Track 28
♩ = 69
C
w/ fingers: m p p m p

Hemiola Effect

By engaging in a *hemiola*—the rhythmic relation of three against two (or four)—your plucking-hand fingers are forced to sound notes in a variety of combinations. Similar to a polyrhythm, the hemiola in **Fig. 29A** arises from our ever-present four-note bass line, plucked against the first-fret C (second string) every three quarter notes. Meanwhile, the hemiola in **Fig. 29B** results from maintaining our familiar bass line while plucking the C every three eighth notes.

Fig. 29A
Track 29
♩ = 69
C
w/ fingers: m p p p m p p m p p m p p

4

Fig. 29B

Track 29

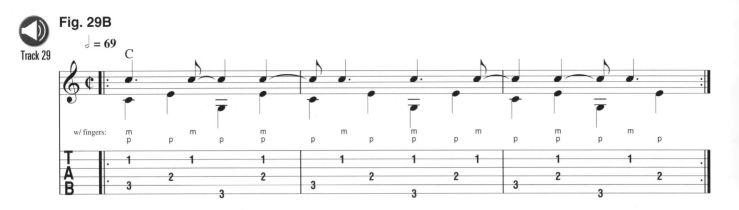

Adding Another String to the Equation

For this next handful of exercises we'll add our plucking-hand's index finger (*i*), using it to sound the open G string in different rhythmic combinations. **Fig. 30A** alternates between our familiar C note on beats 1 and 3, squeezing in our new G note on beats 2 and 4. The roles of these two melody notes are reversed in **Fig. 30B**. Note that these two figures offer no rhythmic independence—both parts are played in quarter notes. The struggle lies in keeping the thumb going to its "proper" string while the second and third strings are plucked in alternation.

Fig. 30A   **Fig. 30B**

Track 30   Track 30

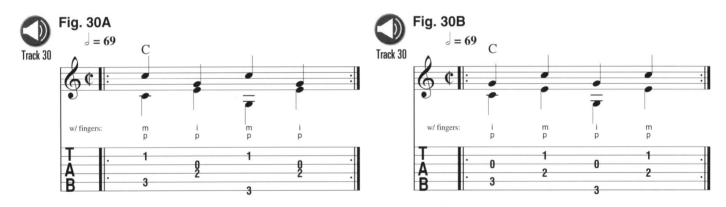

Now let's up the rhythmic ante and unload some eighth notes! Figs. **31A–B** expand upon the previous pair of examples by alternating between the C and G notes at a more rapid rate, plucking two evenly spaced notes per beat!

Fig. 31A   **Fig. 31B**

Track 31   Track 31

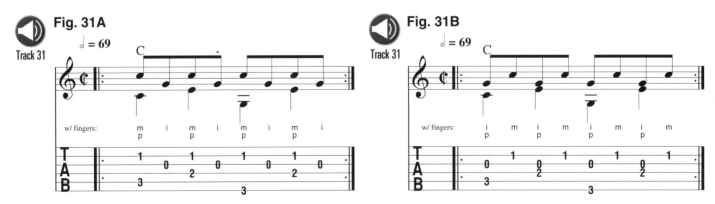

Hemiola Effect Using Two Treble Strings

In **Fig. 32**, our new set of notes is run through the ol' hemiola ringer—akin to Fig. 29B, treble strings are plucked every three eighth notes over our groovy bass line.

Fig. 32

Track 32

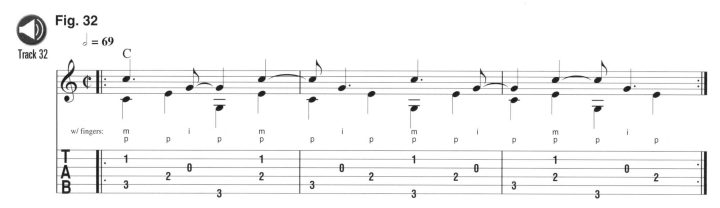

Travis-Picking Pattern #1

Congratulations! If you've gotten this far, you've survived enough rhythmic trickery to start soaking up some interesting Travis-picking patterns. Keep in mind that all of these patterns may also be adapted to other open-chord shapes—just make sure you're grabbing the right chord tones for a functional bass line! (We'll plug these moves into different chords in a moment.)

Fig. 33A illustrates a tasty plucking pattern that features two melody notes. **Fig. 33B** depicts a slight modification: the open high-E string is included for a three-melody-note feel.

Fig. 33A

Track 33

Fig. 33B

Track 33

Travis-Picking Pattern #2

Fig. 34A is another useful Travis-picking pattern using our open-position C chord. Notice that, in this case, the majority of melody notes occur on the upbeats (the "and" of each beat). Meanwhile, in line with the logic of Figs. 33A–B, **Fig. 34B** is a variation that incorporates the open first string—three melody notes for your plucking pleasure!

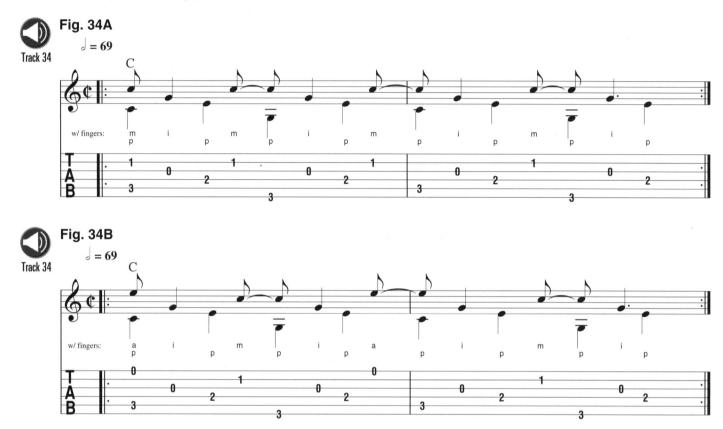

Track 34

Fig. 34A

Fig. 34B

Track 34

Travis-Picking Pattern #3

These next two plucking patterns feature extra notes positioned along various strings, providing more melodic options. In **Fig. 35**, the fretting-hand's fourth finger is used to grab the G note on the high string (third fret). This particular note, a chord tone (G is a C chord's 5th), provides us with a wider range of arpeggio notes from which to draw—different C–E–G notes, spread to the upper reaches of our axe.

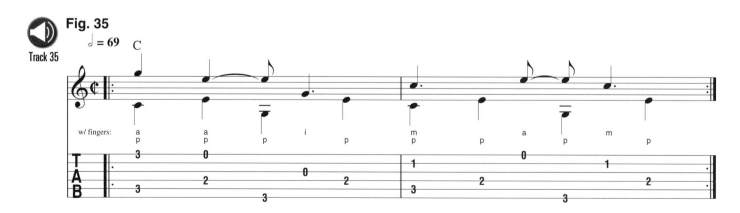

Track 35

Fig. 35

Travis-Picking Pattern #4

A development of the previous example, **Fig. 36** takes our expanded C chord's range (again, featuring a G on the high string) and adds a scale tone—the note D (third fret, second string), fretted with the fourth finger—into its equation. This is the first time we've added a nonchord tone to the mix. As you'll soon see, the more comfortable you get with the basic mechanics of Travis picking, the easier it is to incorporate other scale tones into the picture.

Fig. 36

Track 36

Plugging Travis-Picking Patterns into Progressions

Now let's put some of these moves to the test in a real-life rock/pop progression. **Fig. 37A** flip-flops the measures of Fig. 33A and plugs this "new" move into C–G–Ami–F changes.

Fig. 37A

Track 37

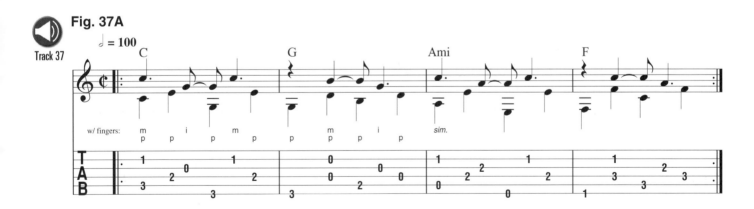

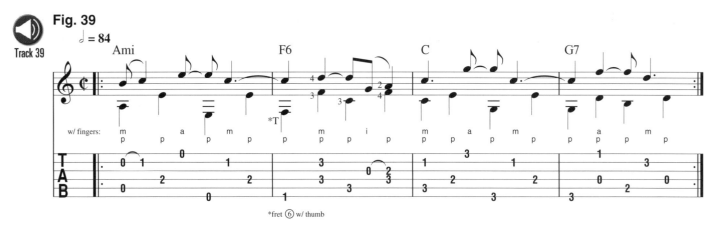

Fig. **37B** is the same progression as the previous example, only with fully fretted chord shapes. Now, all fret-hand fingers need to constantly clamp down on notes, providing a big challenge. In other words, you're bound to find difficulty in keeping melody notes, none of which are open strings, ringing while the alternating bass line keeps moving.

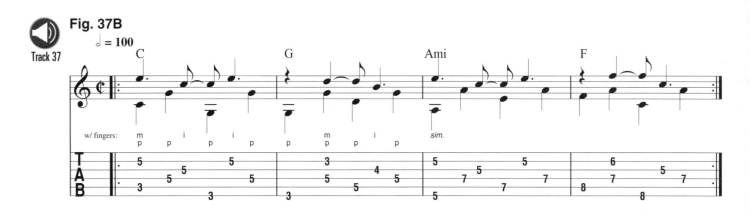

Fig. **38** builds upon the concept of Fig. 36, adding extra notes between chord tones—played with hammer-ons and pull-offs—to create a melody over a C–F change.

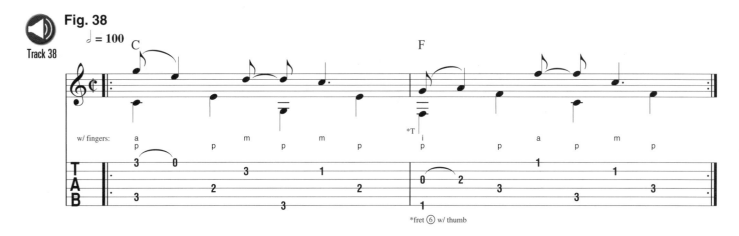

Fig. **39** adds more nonchord tones to the mix, this time over an Ami–F6–C–G7 chord sequence. Note that the hammer-on to A (second fret, third string) coincides with a thumbed F (third fret, fourth string) bass note.

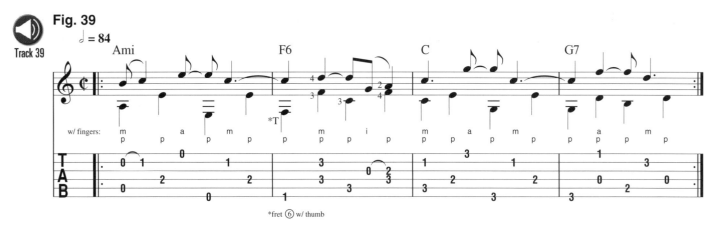

"Solo Interlude" Sample

We'll close out this Travis-picking chapter with **Fig. 40**, a passage that might serve as a "solo interlude" in a mellow rock song. This figure features much melodicism along the upper strings (particularly the second string), phrased with various hammer-ons and pull-offs for maximum ear-pleasing effect. For the last chord, G, slowly rake your plucking-hand's thumb through the indicated notes.

Fig. 40

Track 40

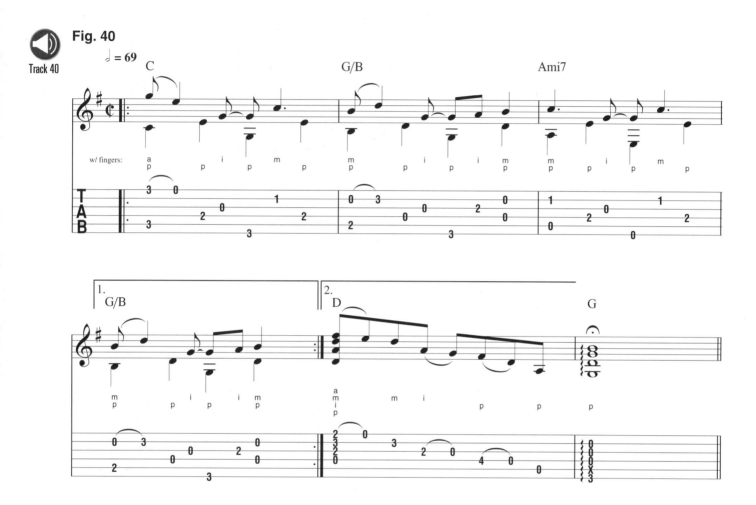

Now that you're grounded in Travis picking, let's turn our attention to another "rootsy" plucking approach—folk-style strumming, as explored in our next chapter. Not only do these new techniques factor into the rockin' styles of your favorite acoustic-rock artists, you'll often find Travis picking combined with these moves to interesting effect.

Folk-Style Strumming

5

In this chapter, we'll study some of the strumming moves used by influential pluckers like Bob Dylan, Joni Mitchell, Joan Baez, and Leonard Cohen, among others—artists who are, at times, loosely classified as "folk." Regardless of the genre with which they're tagged, these artists employ an often-overlooked—at least by rockers—"pick-less strum" sound that's a worthy addition to any contemporary rock or pop singer/songwriter's accompaniment arsenal. Check out the hip accompaniment patterns of pluckers like John Mayer, Elliott Smith, Jeff Buckley, and Eva Cassidy for a few examples. Or look back to the tasty fingerstyle strums that Paul McCartney played in certain Beatles songs. As an added bonus, this section offers two new hand positions—yet another example of trashing classical tradition!

Folk-Style Arpeggio Strums

Before we dive into folk-style strumming, let's explore a "folky" style of arpeggiation that will, inevitably, be used in conjunction with strums. Back in Fig. 40, you were instructed to strum through an entire G chord using the fleshy part of your thumb. This technique has its roots in folk music and comes across as a "gentler" version of what happens when a pick-style player slowly rakes his/her pick through a chord's strings, from low to high. Because each chord's tones are played one after another (albeit very quickly), this is a form of arpeggiation technique. Regardless of whether a pick or fingers are used, this arpeggiated "strum" will be indicated with a *wavy line* alongside a chord's tones in tab and standard notation.

Now let's explore three ways to get the aforementioned sound without using a pick, beginning with **Fig. 41A**, which features some modern adaptations of open chords (i.e., it sounds more "rock"). Here, each chord's tones are quickly "thumb brushed"—that is, the *p* finger is used to gently rake across each chord's tones, from low to high. Interestingly, Elvis Presley used this same technique on his nylon-string while plucking throughout "Love Me Tender." Though each chord is notated in half notes, to make this move sound authentic, begin brushing your thumb across the lower strings *one millisecond before* each chord's designated starting point; you want to hit the *highest note* of each chord exactly on the beat.

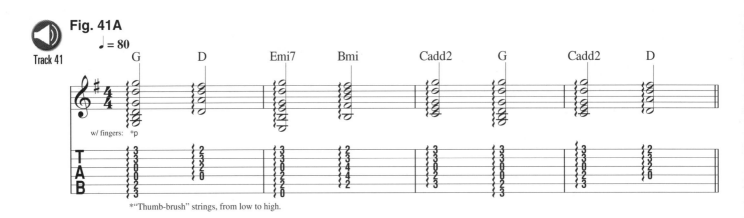

Fig. 41A
Track 41

*"Thumb-brush" strings, from low to high.

Resting Fingertips on Body

It's worth adding that, for stability while doing thumb-brushed arpeggiation, some folky pluckers rest their fingertips on the guitar's body, like the photo below. However, do not use this hand position for any other example in this chapter.

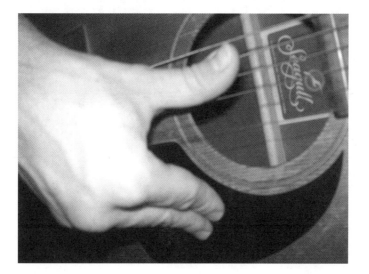

Now compare the sound of Fig. 41A with **Fig. 41B**, a more classical form of arpeggiated strum in which each chord's notes are sounded by quickly rolling each plucking-hand finger (*p–i–m–a*) through indicated strings. Consequently, since we're only plucking with four fingers, unless we do something radical, four notes are the most that we can roll through each chord. Also notice that, compared to Fig. 41A, the end result is a brighter and thinner sound. This is due to the fingertips/nails plucking higher strings and having fewer notes present per chord.

Fig. 41B

Track 41

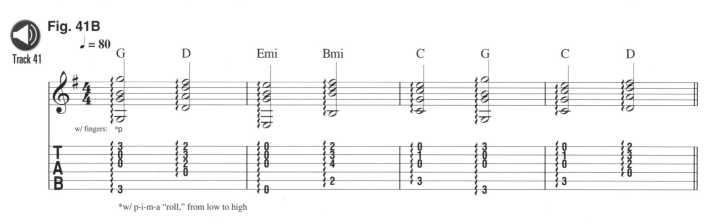

*w/ p-i-m-a "roll," from low to high

Fig. 41C combines the previous two approaches: the thumb (*p*) is used to brush through strings 6–4, while the *i–m–a* fingers pluck strings 3–1, respectively. The two techniques need to work in concert to create an evenly raked arpeggio sound. In this example, the techniques have been rhythmically notated to approximate each arpeggio's timing, as well as to specify the fingers used. Also, a G–F♯ motif on the first string is maintained between changing chords.

Fig. 41C

Track 41

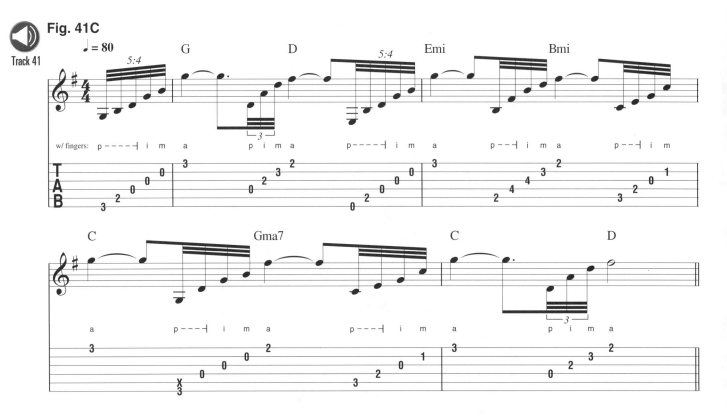

As you practice Figs. 41A–C, take note of the different sounds each technique (or combination there-of) affords. For instance, you might classify Fig. 41A as "warm and mellow," Fig. 41B as "bright and slight-ly thin," while Fig. 41C has a "warm bottom and bright top." That way, you'll be prepared when you come across a musical setting in which only one of the techniques works as the ideal accompaniment.

"Open-Hand" Folk-Style Strumming

In what some refer to as *open-hand* folk-style strumming, the outside portion of the index (*i*), middle (*m*), and ring (*a*) fingers' nails (or fingertip flesh) are used to strum across strings, from low to high. This technique is indicated between notation and tab staves with a directional arrow. For the next few pas-sages, consider using a *heel-down*, or *heel-planting*, plucking-hand position, as seen in the photo below. As you'll soon notice, once we start mixing open-hand strums with arpeggiation and Travis-picking tech-niques, this hand position yields more stability and accuracy, as well as overall comfort.

When using this new hand position, the "starting" and "ending" movements for open-hand folk-style strumming should look like the photos below:

Heel-Planting Stability Position

Fingers After Open-Hand Strum

Fig. 42 presents some open-hand folk-style strums in conjunction with thumb-plucked bass notes.

Fig. 42

Track 42

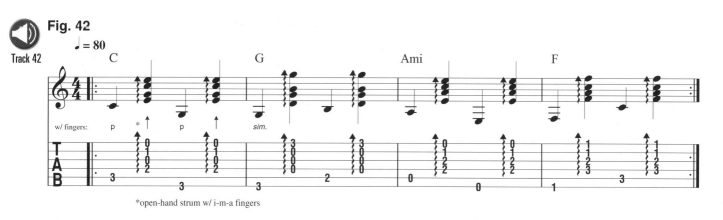

*open-hand strum w/ i-m-a fingers

For the next several examples, we'll be experimenting with open-hand strums in *both* directions, using the index (*i*), middle (*m*), and ring (*a*) fingers' nails (or fingertip flesh) to strum across strings, from low to high, then reverse the motion, resulting in eighth-note strums with the fingertips.

Figs. 43A–B offer two takes on an alternating (down/up) open-hand strum. You can hear these types of moves in the Beatles' "Mother Nature's Son," among countless other songs. The key to making these figures sound "right" is the placement of accents (>) on beats 2 and 4. Outwardly "explode" your fingers a little more aggressively at these points so that the chords "pop" at a louder volume. Accents add an extra groove element, making these folky passages rock!

Fig. 43A

Track 43

Fig. 43B

Track 43

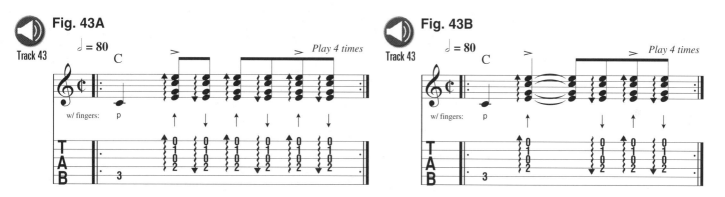

Fig. 44A plugs Fig. 43A's preliminary move into a sequence of colorful chords, all featuring a G note (third fret, first string) voiced on top. Also, notice the moving "voice" along the second string—it shifts back-and-forth between D (measures 1 and 3) and C (measures 2 and 4). Meanwhile, **Fig. 44B** explores a D–C–B–C motif along the second string, using Fig. 43B's plucking pattern.

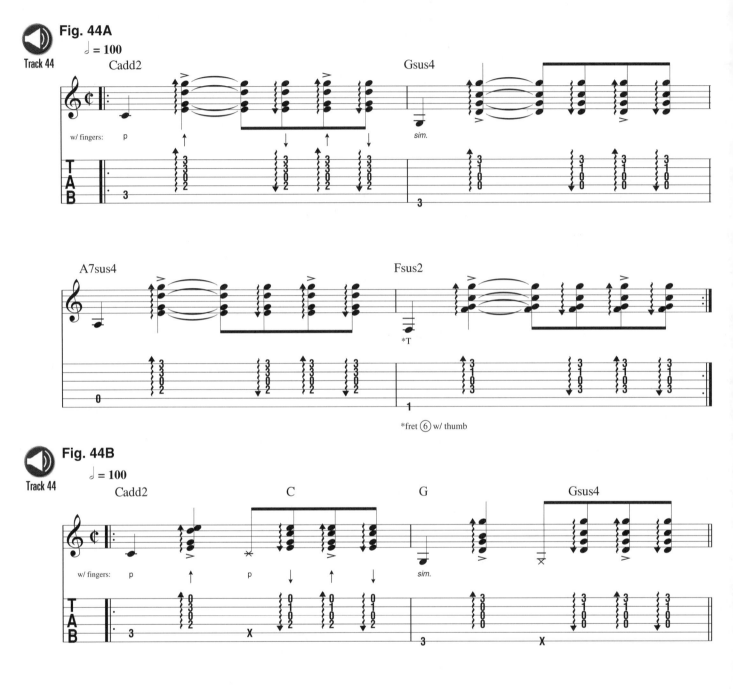

*fret ⑥ w/ thumb

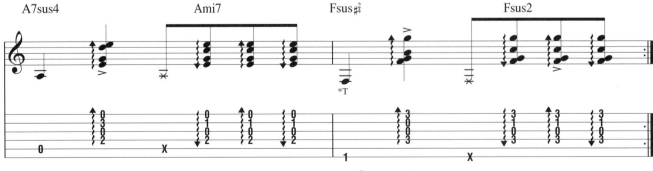

*fret ⑥ w/ thumb

Homage to Elliott Smith

The most interesting fingerstyle figures use a hybrid of this chapter's techniques, as well as other approaches we've studied thus far. In the opinion of many, no acoustic plucker in the rock realm excels at this craft more than singer/songwriter Elliott Smith did. We'll close out this chapter with a couple of examples in his style, beginning with **Fig. 45**, which is modeled after Smith's "Angeles" and mixes folk-style strums with rapid Travis-picked arpeggios.

Fig. 45

Track 45

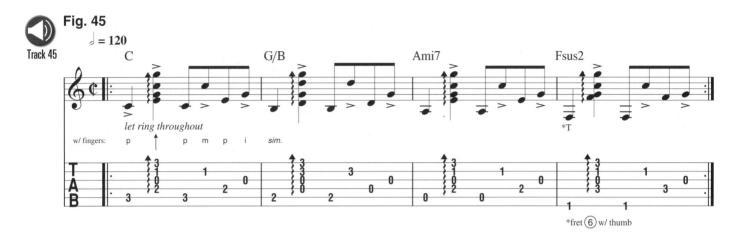

Smith also favored folk-style double-strums like those used in Figs. 43–44. You can hear his mastery of open-hand strums—used in both directions—mixed with single-note melody riffs on lower strings in songs like "Southern Belle," à la **Fig. 46**.

Fig. 46

Track 46

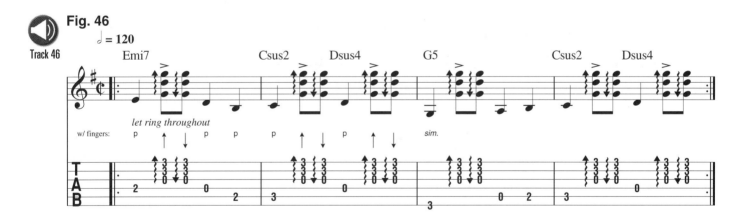

Open-Chord Ornaments

6

So far, we've studied *piano-style plucking*, for parts combining bass and chord partials; numerous *arpeggios*, to mix up notes within individual chords; and *Travis picking* and *folk-style strums*, to gain a deeper understanding of moves favored by 1960s–'70s rock artists, and those of whom they've influenced. We've also significantly enhanced our arsenal of *chord voicings*—various ways to play an open C, G, Ami, or F chord, among others. In many cases, these fresh voicings were the result of adding/subtracting certain notes to/from standard open-position chords. This chapter explores this concept in greater detail, focusing on specific tones that you can employ, this time using hammer-ons and/or pull-offs. In other words, we'll study—in depth—how to add *single-note ornaments* to common chord shapes. This technique is key to moving beyond using the same, old arpeggio patterns and other fixed-chord techniques (this will be the first time that we don't apply the same plucking pattern to each chord within a progression) every time you pluck open-position "cowboy" chords on your acoustic guitar.

James Taylor is widely regarded as the ultimate "open-chord ornament" acoustic plucker. But as you'll soon see—and hear—these sounds surface in every conceivable acoustic guitar style, not just folk-based rock and pop, and are a mainstay in the recorded work of revered pluckers ranging from Eric Clapton and Jimmy Page to comparative newcomers like John Mayer, Joseph Arthur, Elliott Smith, John Frusciante, Damien Rice, and others. And let's not leave the ladies out! Icons like Ani DiFranco, Jewel, Lisa Loeb, Sarah McLachlan, and Shawn Colvin also make it standard practice to avoid playing obvious fingerstyle patterns, instead, ornamenting their open-chord shapes with hammered and pulled moves. Let's run our hands through a few purely physical examples (without the theory explanation) so you can hear ornaments in action; then we'll go in depth, approaching things on a chord-by-chord basis.

Folk-Rock Travis-Picking Pattern with Open-Chord Ornaments

Fig. 47 is a Travis-picking passage in which each chord starts off with a hammer-on from B (open, second string) to C (first fret, second string), plucked simultaneously with a bass note. This hammer-on is the ornament, and its use throughout the entire chord sequence creates a melodic "hook." The progression and plucking-hand pattern are similar to what Bob Dylan uses in "Don't Think Twice, It's Alright."

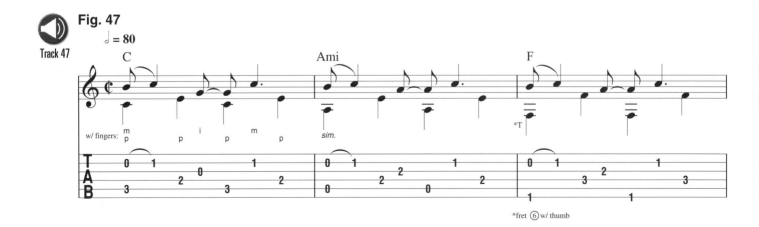

Fig. 47
Track 47
♩ = 80

*fret ⑥ w/ thumb

Open-String Exploitation

If your guitar's open strings (E–A–D–G–B–E) are all *diatonic* to the key you're playing in (meaning they're part of that key's scale), you can hammer on to fretted notes from them, like **Fig. 48**. Notice that, regardless of the strings plucked in each four-note chord, the *p–i–m–a* fingers are rolled from low to high.

Fig. 48
Track 48

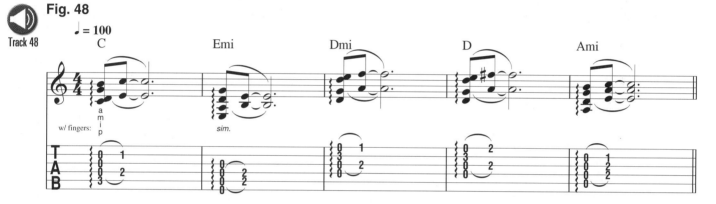

Entry-Level Chord Decorations: Sus4 and Sus2 Sounds

Now let's look at these types of figures from a more "scientific" standpoint (i.e., describe the function of specific tones we add to certain voicings) so that we may apply their formulas to other chords in improvised accompaniment.

Figs. **49A–B** take a basic open C chord (C–E–G) and interject a "2" (D) and "4" (F). Whenever a chord's 3rd (e.g., the note E in a C chord) is replaced with a "2" or a "4," an unresolved, *suspended* sound results; hence, you get chord names like Csus2 (C–D–G) and Csus4 (C–F–G). Check out how these tones are used in the following arpeggiated figures, which feature hammer-ons and pull-offs.

Fig. 49A
Track 49

Fig. 49B
Track 49

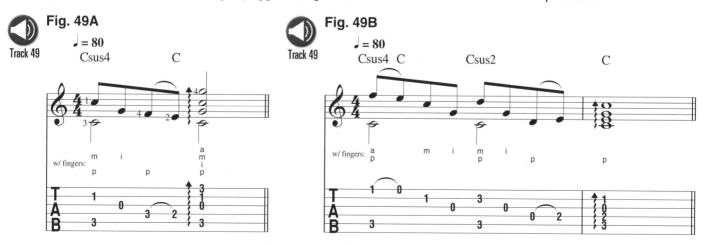

Applying Suspension to Open D and Open A Chords

The next several figures depict basic open chords, colorized with suspended tones that are hammered on or pulled off. Now read this: It's important to realize that, for your own improvisational and compositional skills, sus2 and sus4 sounds can be resolved to *both* major and minor chords. For example, a Dsus4 (D–G–A) or Dsus2 (D–E–A) chord can just as easily be resolved to Dmi (D–F–A) or D (D–F♯–A), as in **Figs. 50A–B**, respectively. You just need to know which kind of D chord fits in the key that you're playing. Likewise, Asus4 (A–D–E) or Asus2 (A–B–E) can be resolved to Ami (A–C–E) or A (A–C♯–E), like **Figs. 51A–B**, respectively.

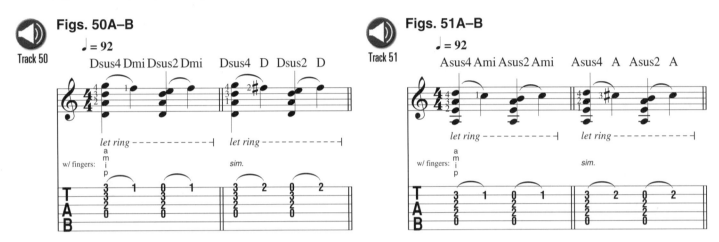

Applying Suspension to Open G and Open F Chords

Since there aren't any basic open versions of Gmi and Fmi, Gsus4 (G–C–D) and Gsus2 (G–A–D) are resolved to G (G–B–D) in **Figs. 52A–B**, respectively, and Fsus4 (F–B♭–C) and Fsus2 (F–G–C) are resolved to F (F–A–C) in **Figs. 53A–B**. Notice the "homemade" G chord fingering in Fig. 52B, which was required to make a hammer-on possible between the sus2 (A) and the chord's 3rd (B). Never fear experimenting in this fashion; from solving problems like this, you'll doubtlessly create some usable moves of your own.

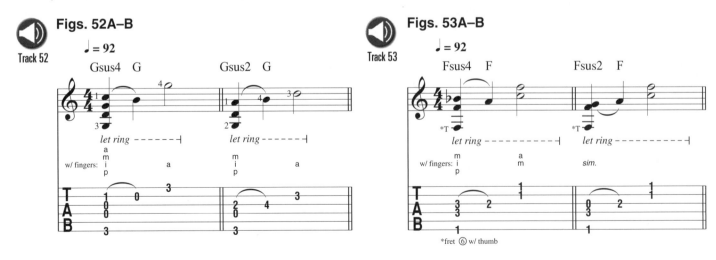

Applying Suspension to Open E Chords

Figs. 54A–D show some different possibilities for resolving to Emi (E–G–B) or E (E–G♯–B) chords from Esus2 (E–F♯–B) and Esus4 (E–A–B) sounds.

Figs. 54A–B

Track 54

Figs. 54C–D

Track 54

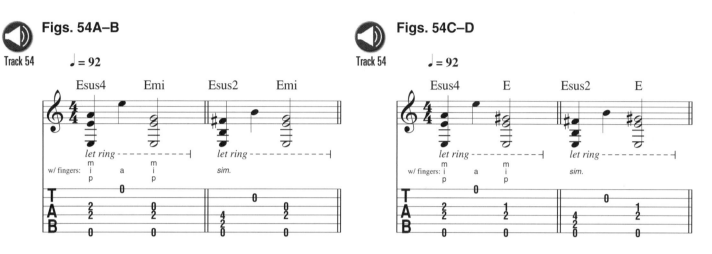

Applying Suspension to B and F♯ Chords

These next figures focus on "second tier" open-position shapes—chords like B minor and B major and F♯ minor and F♯ major, which you're bound to come across, provided you're plucking in major (or related minor) keys. Towards that end, **Figs. 55A–B** show some different possibilities for resolving Bsus4 (B–E–F♯) to Bmi (B–D–F♯) and B (B–D♯–F♯) chords; **Figs. 56A–B** resolve F♯sus4 (F♯–B–C♯) to F♯mi (F♯–A–C♯) and F♯ (F♯–A♯–C♯).

Figs. 55A–B

Track 55

Figs. 56A–B

Track 56

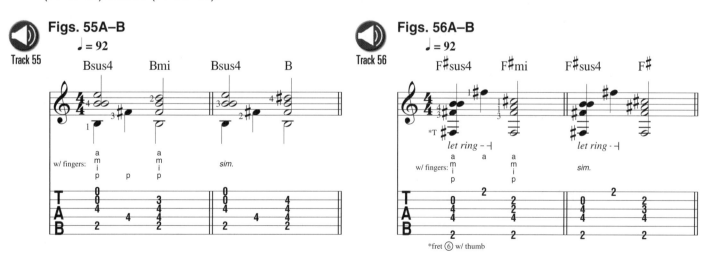

Using Double Suspensions

This last suspended example [**Fig. 57**] embellishes a C–Ami–Dmi–G change with *double suspensions*—replacing an upper register root and 3rd with a 2 *and* 4, respectively—and their resolution. For example, in the opening measure, an open C chord's highest root (C; first fret, second string) and 3rd (E; open, first string) are replaced with D (third fret, second string) and F (first fret, first string), respectively, then resolved to the standard C chord. The remaining chords are similarly ornamented.

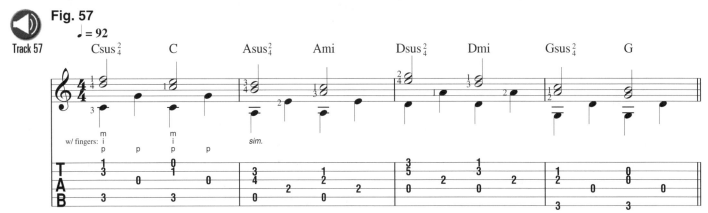

Open-Chord Ornaments Using Pentatonics and Suspensions

Now let's put the aforementioned added tones to work, using them—and, in many cases, a chord's related *pentatonic* scale—to create some hip open sounds. We'll also beef up the music-theory and analysis lingo, which, if theory is relatively new to you, may help "connect the dots," as well as fingering details.

Open E Chord

Fig. 58 adds one extra note (A; second fret, third string) to a garden-variety open-E arpeggio pattern. Since the fret hand's first, second, and third fingers are already grabbing the chord's primary notes (E–G♯–B), the fourth finger will be used in quick hammer-on fashion to color this chord. In analysis of the E major scale (E–F♯–G♯–A–B–C♯–D♯), you can see by counting scale steps that "A" is the 4th degree of the scale. Again, whenever a chord's 3rd (in this case, G♯) is replaced by a 4th (in this case, A) a sus4 (suspended 4th) sound results. This note functions as a "suspension" because it "suspends" a chord's resolution, temporarily avoiding settling into a clear-cut major (E) or minor (Emi) tonality. Some plucked harmonics, an unfailingly tasty sound on acoustic guitar, punctuate this passage.

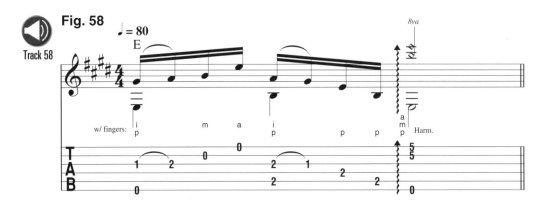

Note: Make every effort to keep *all* of your fingers anchored throughout, adding and subtracting only the fourth finger. Perform all other examples to similar effect (e.g., keep fingers depressed as much as possible).

Open G Chord

By grabbing the root of an open G chord (third fret, sixth string) with the fret hand's third finger (keeping it anchored throughout), remaining digits become available to add all sorts of ornaments to this shape. In **Fig. 59**, the first finger pulls off from C (first fret, second string) to the open B string. Meanwhile, the second finger hammers on extra tones: E (second fret, fourth string) and B (second fret, fifth string). Within the G major scale (G–A–B–C–D–E–F♯), this hammer-on/pull-off activity adds the sus4 (C), 2nd (the open A string), and 6th (E) to a G triad (G–B–D), imparting a G major pentatonic (G–A–B–D–E) flavor. In addition to the ever-present sus4, in later examples you'll see how notes from a chord's related pentatonic scale (G major pentatonic over G, C major pentatonic over C, A minor pentatonic over Ami, etc.) are invaluable assets when ornamenting open chords.

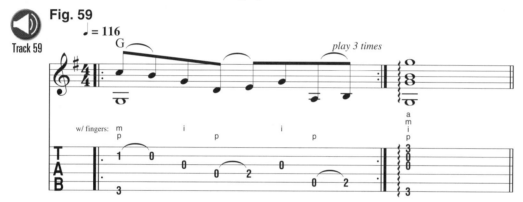

Fig. 59

♩ = 116

Track 59

Open D Chord

In **Fig. 60**'s D chord example, somewhat inspired by James Taylor's "Sweet Baby James," the fret hand's fourth and second fingers are added/subtracted to/from core tones (D–F♯–A), playing a sus4 (G; third fret, first string) and E (open, first string) with hammer-ons and pull-offs, respectively; related to the D major scale (D–E–F♯–G–A–B–C♯), these are the second (E) and fourth (G) scale degrees. While the fret hand's remaining fingers (first and third) hold down the D chord's remaining pitches, the thumb (T) is employed to play F♯ (second fret, sixth string) on the downbeat of measure 2. If you find it difficult to hammer on and/or pull off the notes along the high E string while this chord is held, check to be sure that your third finger's tip is fretting *straight down* on the string; otherwise that fingertip's pad might unintentionally come into contact with the first string, making pull-offs unnecessarily difficult.

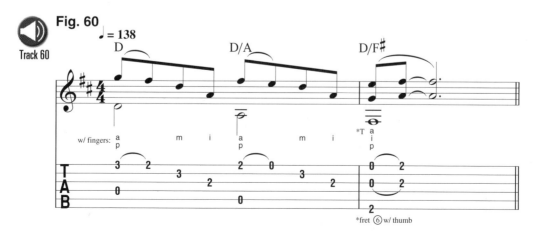

Fig. 60

♩ = 138

Track 60

*fret ⑥ w/ thumb

Open C Chord

From a performance perspective, you've likely noticed that the figures in this section all work as great song-ending moves, among other things. This next passage is no exception!

Fig. 61's C-chord example keeps both C notes (first fret, second string; third fret, fifth string) depressed throughout (using the fret hand's first and third fingers), while the fourth and second fingers get tied in knots while fretting the D (third fret, second string), F (third fret, fourth string), and A (second fret, third string) pitches. These maneuvers add the ol' sus4 (F), as well as C major pentatonic pitches (C–D–E–G–A), to a basic C chord (C–E–G).

Fig. 61

Track 61

Open Ami Chord

Interestingly, Ami (A–C–E) can be embellished using an approach similar to the one used for the C chord in the previous example. Only in this case, in **Fig. 62**, we'll use pitches from the Ami chord's related A minor pentatonic scale (A–C–D–E–G), and the fret hand's fourth finger to tack on D (third fret, second string), and third and second fingers to hammer on from the open third (G) and fourth (D) strings, respectively.

Fig. 62

Track 62

Open Dmi Chord

In **Fig. 63**, while all the notes of an open Dmi chord are held down, the open E string is sounded via a pull-off from F, at the first string's first fret, and the A on the third string (second fret) is preceded by a hammer-on from the open G string. This adds the 2nd (E) and 4th (G) scale degrees to our Dmi sound, all within the D natural minor scale (D–E–F–G–A–B♭–C). Interestingly, this Lindsey Buckingham–like figure (akin to "Big Love") sounds not unlike certain Travis-picking patterns we studied a few chapters back.

Fig. 63

Track 63

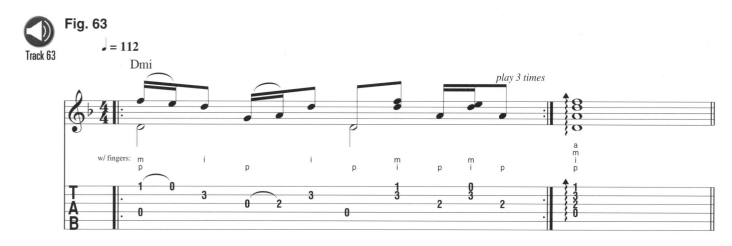

Open A Chord

Measure 1 of **Fig. 64** illustrates a James Taylor–like treatment of a basic A chord (A–C♯–E). Finger this chord, from low to high, using your second, third, and fourth fingers, otherwise the hammer-ons/pull-offs to/from the open B string won't be playable. (Note: James Taylor actually plays this A-chord shape so that his *first* finger can be used to hammer on/pull off along the second string, fretting it, from low to high, with his second, third, and first fingers!) The fourth finger also needs to be shifted along the second string to grab C♯ (second fret, second string) *and* D (third fret, second string). At measure 2, shift hand positions, using a first-finger barre across the second fret. This frees up the frethand's second finger to hammer on and pull off the D note (third fret, second string) and fourth finger for a stretch up to a high A (fifth fret, first string). All in all, we've just tacked on the 2nd (B) and 4th (D) degrees of the A major scale (A–B–C♯–D–E–F♯–G♯) to our original A chord.

Fig. 64

Track 64

Open Emi Chord

Fig. 65's E minor chord example might cause some problems for you, as it requires a different set of plucking-hand fingers from what we've used in other chord-ornament moves. Here, the ring (*a*) and middle (*m*) fingers tackle two string pairs (strings 1–2 and 2–3), while the index finger (*i*) plucks notes on the fourth string. As usual, the thumb (*p*) plays strings 5–6.

To pluck this passage properly, grab Emi (E–G–B) in customary fashion, fretting the B (second fret, fifth string) and E (second fret, fourth string) notes with your second and third fingers, respectively. While those notes are held down, the fourth finger frets/pulls off the extra pitches—A (second fret, third string), G (third fret, first string), and F♯ (second fret, first string). The fret hand's second finger also tosses in a tasty hammer-on to the E chord's B (second fret, fifth string) from the open A string. All of this activity outlines the E minor hexatonic scale (E–F♯–G–A–B–D), a six-note E minor scale that omits the ♭6 scale degree (in this case, C) from E natural minor (E–F♯–G–A–B–C–D).

Fig. 65

Putting It All Together

Fig. 66 juggles many of the previously studied chords and their respective ornaments in an Ami–F–C–G progression. All totaled, this figure substitutes an Ami7 for a mundane Ami, an Fsus2 for a boring F, and adds tasty embellishments into the mix; essentially, each chord is spruced up with hammer-on and/or pull-off ornaments stemming from the pentatonic scale that relates directly to each chord's root: A minor pentatonic (A–C–D–E–G) over Am7, F major pentatonic (F–G–A–C–D) over Fsus2, C major pentatonic (C–D–E–G–A) over C, and G major pentatonic (G–A–B–D–E) over G. (On the CD, double stops and triple stops are played with open-hand strums on the figure's repeat to illustrate a different effect with the same notes.) Keep this concept in mind and improvise your own accompaniment through the progression.

Fig. 66

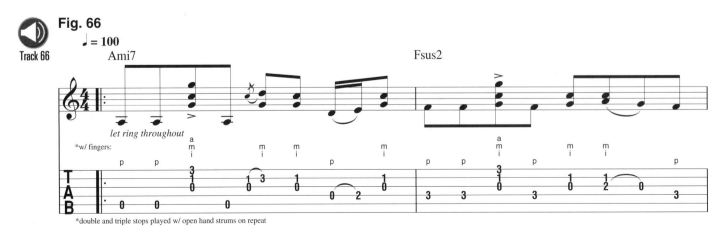

*double and triple stops played w/ open hand strums on repeat

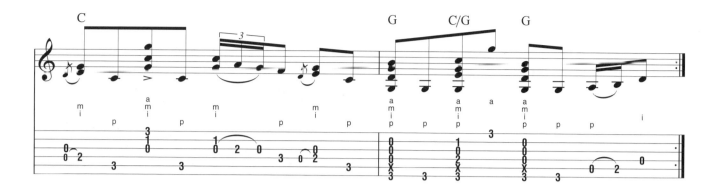

Creating Your Own Signature Fingerstyle Riffs

If you're a songwriter, or collaborate with others as a member of a band's rhythm section, it's essential that you learn how to combine different voicings, plucking-hand techniques, and ornamental moves without creating musical distraction. For instance, don't just cram random approaches into a song's chorus simply because you've been practicing some new things. Find out where the vocal melody sits in the song by *listening*, and then fill in the unoccupied space.

To get an idea of what goes on behind the scenes during the creation of cool fingerstyle parts, check out **Figs. 67A–D**, which include all of the different elements, presented one piece at a time, that factor into a usable figure (cumulatively heard in Fig. 67D). **Fig. 67A** immediately clarifies the harmony via a complete-chord statement on the downbeat, using a technique we learned in Fig. 48; **Fig. 67B** shows how the role of the bass can be beefed up, not unlike approaches we used earlier in our piano-style chapter; **Fig. 67C** inserts an upper-register common tone (G; third fret, first string), a key component in rock-sounding acoustic accompaniment; and **Fig. 67D** adds the finishing touch—an open-string ornament, working as a "fill" on beat 4 of each measure. All totaled, you have a multidimensional part that adds subtle rhythmic and melodic interest, yet stays out of the way of the real focal point, the vocalist, and complements the song.

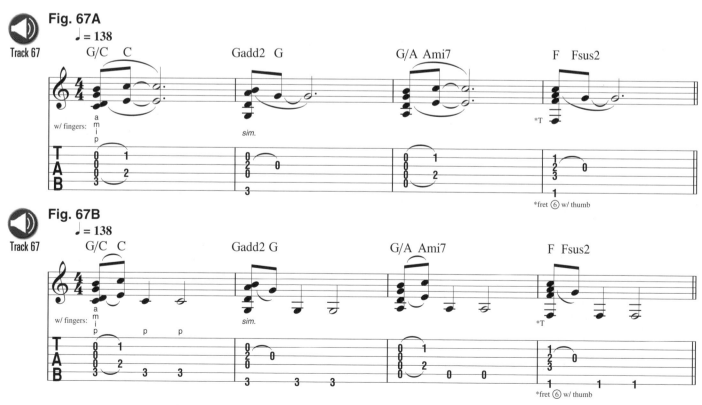

Fig. 67C

Track 67

♩ = 138

Fig. 67D

Track 67

♩ = 138

*fret ⑥ w/thumb

Dominant 7th Chord Sounds

As we've discussed in previous chapters, the dominant 7th chord is probably one of the least "rock-sounding" 7th chords you'll come across, especially when played as a fully fretted barre chord. Dominant 7th barre chords just sound more at home in blues, country, funk, and varieties of R&B. When played in open position, however, the dominant 7th chord does lend itself to all sorts of classic-rock sounds. Let's close out this chapter by adding a few ornaments to some open-position dominant 7th shapes.

Open B7 Chord

Fig. 68 is a B7-based (B–D♯–F♯–A) Travis-picking passage that features an alternating root–3rd–5th bass line and melodic movement on the first and second strings. The fret hand's second finger grabs B (second fret, fifth string) and F♯ (second fret, sixth string) in alternation; the fourth finger pulls off from a high F♯ (second fret, first string) to the open E, then executes a microtonal (i.e., quarter-step) bend on the second string; and your first and third fingers remain steadfastly rooted on D♯ (first fret, fourth string) and A (second fret, third string), respectively.

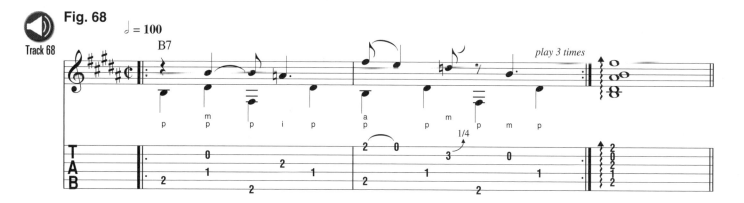

Fig. 68

Track 68

Open A7, D7, and G7 Moves

In the guitar work of singer/songwriters like Jeff Buckley ("What Will You Say"), Elliott Smith ("Color Bars"), and John Lennon ("Woman"), open-position dominant shapes are often plucked, or strummed with the open hand, in syncopated eighth notes and decorated with notes outside the chords, like **Figs. 69A–C**. Here, nonchord tones—primarily the 2 and 4, replacing a chord's 3rd and, again, creating suspension—are grabbed on higher strings with available fret hand fingers, while the rest of the chords remain intact. For clarity, fret hand fingerings are specified next to each chord's notehead throughout.

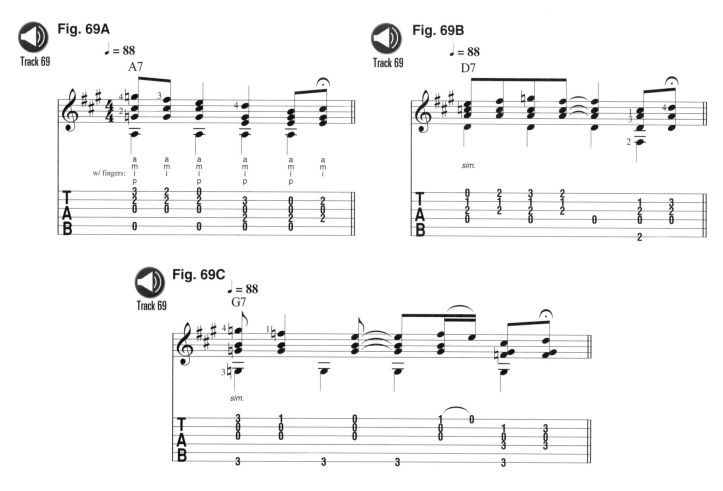

Fig. 69A

Track 69

Fig. 69B

Track 69

Fig. 69C

Track 69

Of course, all of the ornamental approaches in this chapter can also be used with fully fretted chords; it's just much more difficult, due to the fact that we only have five fret hand fingers! Nevertheless, we'll torture ourselves in this area soon, so keep your eyes peeled.

Pedal Point and Inversion

7

Numerous figures that we've plucked through so far have taken on a modern edge due to the use of upper-register common tones, a single note maintained atop changing chords. Though we have not described them as such, this is technically referred to as *inverted pedal point*. **Fig. 70** is a hip example in E minor to remind you of this sound, as is the thumb-brushed **Fig. 71** (not unlike the voicings explored way back in Fig. 7).

All totaled, there are three forms of pedal point, all of which are useful in creating cool rock fingerstyle moves: *tonic pedal*, *internal pedal*, and *inverted pedal*. We'll test-drive these sounds, and then describe the effect that the "pedal approach" has on certain chords.

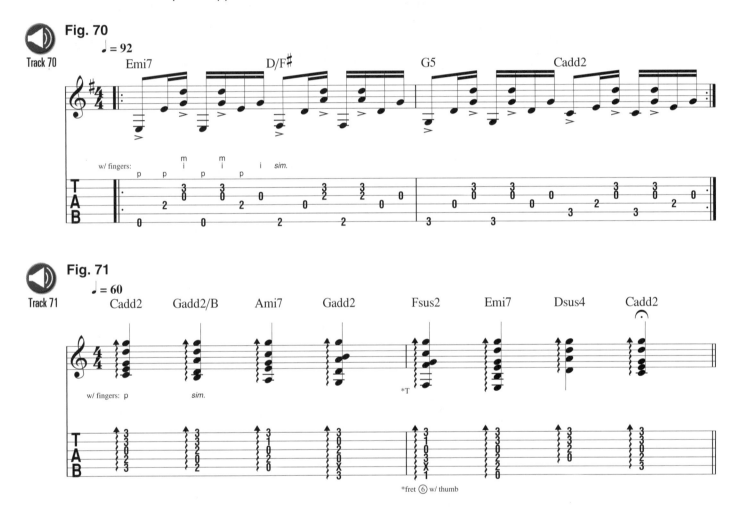

Tonic Pedal Point

If you've played through acoustic-driven songs like the Who's "Substitute," you know how hip moving the fretted notes of an open D chord up the neck sounds. **Fig. 72A** illustrates a similar effect; the open D string is thumb-plucked repeatedly while three-note chords are popped out with the *i–m–a* fingers. In this case, regardless of the chords voiced on top, the tonal center—or *tonic*—is D major. Hence, this is an example of *tonic pedal point*. The Who's Pete Townshend also used similar moves over an A tonic pedal in "I Can't Explain," approximated for fingerstyle guitar in **Fig. 72B**.

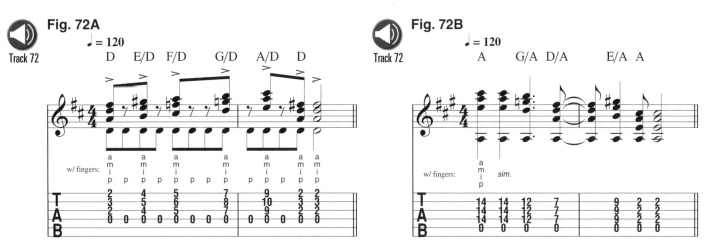

Slash Chords: Voicing Triads over Fixed Bass Notes

No, a *slash chord* doesn't have anything to do with a certain GN'R/Velvet Revolver top hat–wearing picker—though Slash certainly plays 'em! Slash chords are simply voicings with a note other than that chord's root in the low register, the specific bass note written to the right of a slash (/). The slash chords in **Figs. 73A–D** are also called *inversions* because the bass note is part of the original chord, specifically A/E (A–C#–E), C/G (C–E–G), D/A (D–F#–A), and F/C (F–A–C).

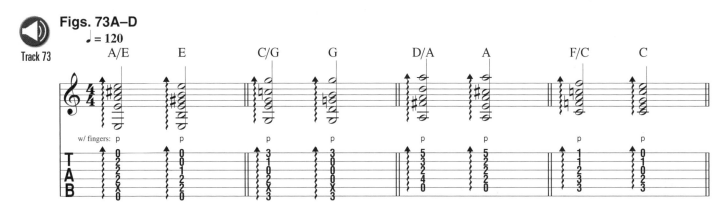

The previous open-position moves featured fixed bass notes on the fifth or sixth strings, a sound derivative of acoustic-based Neil Young ("Sugar Mountain") and Eagles ("Take It Easy") tunes, among others. **Fig. 74A** puts these voicings to work in a two-bar riff using a C tonic pedal throughout; **Fig. 74B** features similar sounds using fully fretted chords, not unlike an acoustic fingerstyle version of Keith Richards' chord vamps with the Rolling Stones.

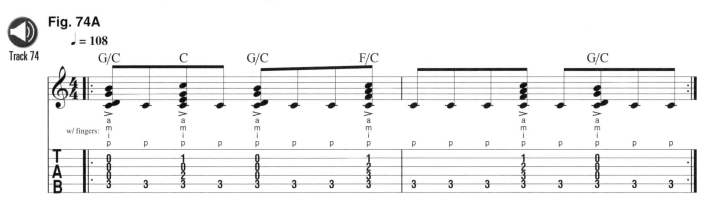

Fig. 74B

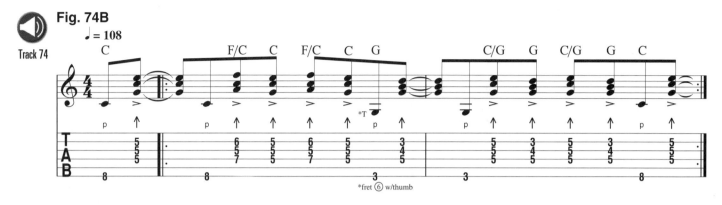

More Inverted Open Chords

In your experience with open chords, you've doubtlessly encountered times in which shapes like C and Ami were approached and/or connected in a progression with a chord like G/B—a G chord with its 3rd (B) in the bass. This inversion (G/B) helps create a stepwise bass line between the aforementioned chords, as in **Fig. 75A**. **Fig. 75B** similarly connects G and Emi open shapes via D/F#—a D chord with its 3rd (F#) in the bass. Incidentally, the chord moves in both examples are punctuated with lengthy *rests*. For these moments of musical silence, loosen your fret hand's grip (this is known as *chord choking*), and simultaneously cover the strings by putting your plucking hand in "planting" position (see Chapter 1).

Fig. 75A **Fig. 75B**

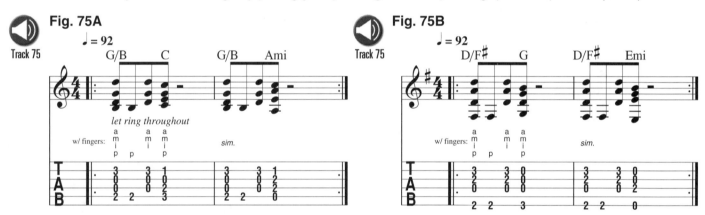

Inverted Barre Chords

In advanced acoustic-rock styles—instances in which the guitar provides piano-style accompaniment, or you just need to grab shapes that don't exist near the nut—you'll need to get busy with fully fretted versions of inverted chords. For these, check out **Figs. 76A–C**—inversions of C, G, Ami, and F chords with the fret hand's thumb on the sixth string that are used to achieve smooth *voice leading* (i.e., minimal movement between notes as chords change).

Figs. 76A–C

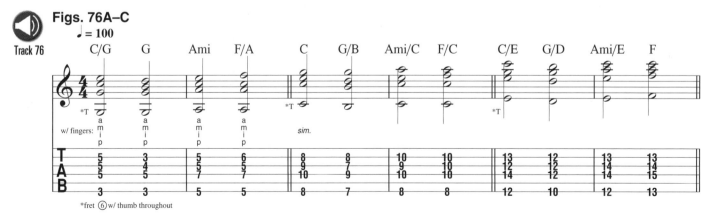

More Inversions in Action: Open and Fully Fretted Examples

Figs. **77A–B** illustrate two takes on an arpeggiated riff, both featuring inversions that yield a stepwise bass line, and plucked in open and closed positions, respectively.

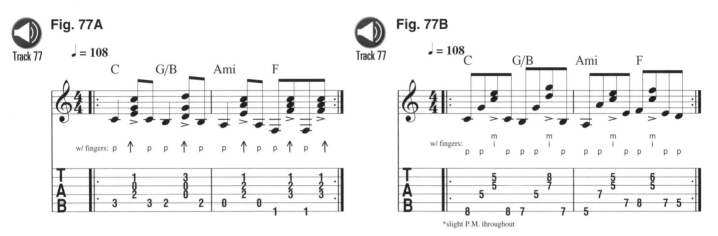

Fig. 77A
Track 77

Fig. 77B
Track 77

*slight P.M. throughout

Internal Pedal: Droning Middle Strings

Anytime you're playing a passage like **Fig. 78A**—a riff containing fixed notes in the *middle register* (here, the open G string) of an evolving harmonic texture (here, moving bass notes and 10th intervals)—you're using an *internal pedal*. This open-G-string-drone approach to pedal point was made famous by Paul McCartney in the Beatles' "Blackbird," and is played mostly in the key of G, using notes from the G major scale (G–A–B–C–D–E–F♯). **Fig. 78B** demonstrates another take on this, modified for the key of C, using notes from the C major scale (C–D–E–F–G–A–B). Try making up some of your own "Blackbird"-inspired figures, sticking to the notes of the aforementioned scales.

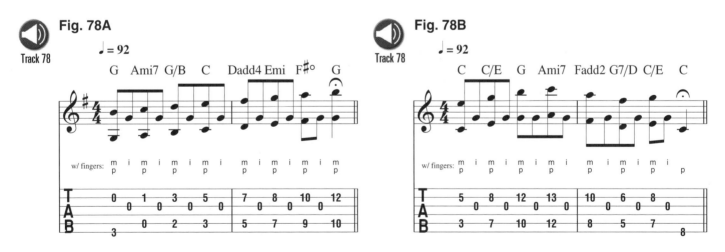

Fig. 78A
Track 78

Fig. 78B
Track 78

Beyond "Blackbird"

Though "Blackbird"-styled passages are enjoyable to pluck, almost every musician inspired by this approach plays them in standard keys like G and C. Truth be told, *any* open string can be used as a drone in this fashion, and *any* key can be used, provided that the open string is part of the key's corresponding scale. For example, **Fig. 79A** drones the open G string for a C minor figure, using notes exclusively from the C natural minor scale (C–D–E♭–F–G–A♭–B♭); **Fig. 79B** drones the open B string, and is fashioned from notes in E major (E–F♯–G♯–A–B–C♯–D♯).

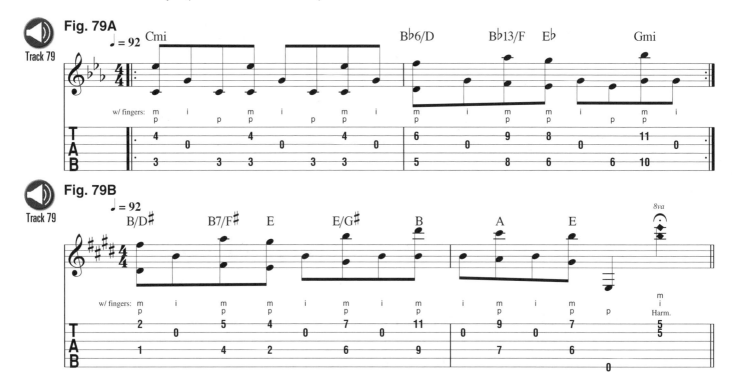

Nicking Moves from Nick Drake

Fig. 80 is reminiscent of Nick Drake's mellow acoustic plucking. Note how our amped-up "Blackbird" approach—this time, the open D string used amidst a variety of shapes derived from G minor (G–A–B♭–C–D–E♭–F)—creates the illusion that an open tuning is being employed. In general, sprinkling open strings into the mix with fully fretted notes—grabbed in the middle of the neck and higher—creates all sorts of interesting "fake open tuning" sounds. (Notice that this passage suggests using the *i* and *m* fingers in unusual spots, swapping/reswapping roles on strings 2–3.)

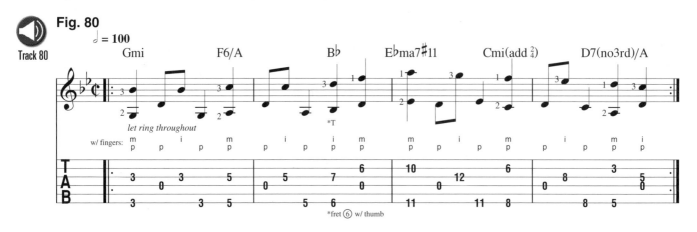

More on "Faking" Open Tunings

Singer/songwriter Jeff Buckley is also known for his colorful chord structures, many of which stem from various forms of using a pedal point, a sound often mistaken for an open tuning. In **Fig. 81A**, an octave shape is shifted along strings 3 and 5, while strings 1, 2, and 6 resonate, creating an ethereal effect. This is actually a form of *oblique motion*—where one voice moves (the octave) while others (the open strings) remain unchanged—with a tonic pedal (E). Use your thumb to pluck the sixth string and an open-hand strum for higher strings. **Fig. 81B** features Buckley's approach to *shell voicings*—seventh chords (Ema7, G#mi7, C#mi7, Ama7, etc.) containing only the root, 3rd, and 7th—intermingled with the open E and B strings. Again, the unchanging notes (the open first and second strings) sound in the middle register for more internal pedal. (Yes, they're the "top" strings, but in this voicing most of the fretted notes ring higher.)

Fig. 81A

Track 81

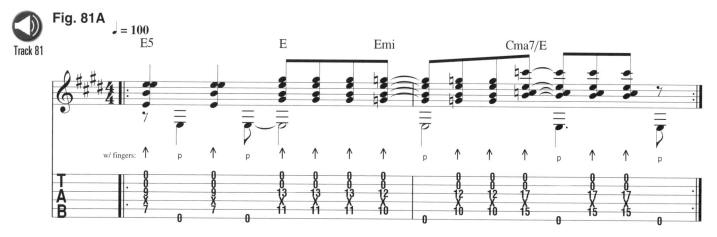

Fig. 81B

Track 81

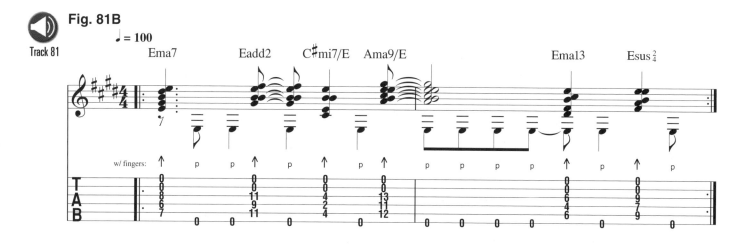

Percussive Approaches

8

This section covers different ways your plucking-hand fingers can add *percussive effects*—sounds that elevate a passage's rhythmic intensity—to your acoustic playing. In some ways, you want to think like a drummer: Hits from a snare could be "popping" sounds plucked on middle strings, kick-drum thumps could be reproduced via aggressively thumbed bass notes, and the textural wash or syncopation from cymbals and hi-hats might be mimicked with repeated droning of the upper strings. For example, a basic drum-set groove, as it translates to guitar, could be the combinations of thumbed bass notes (the kick/bass drum), E notes on beats 2 and 4 (à la the snare), and steady eighth or sixteenth notes plucked on high strings (the hi-hat), like **Figs. 82A–B**. (Note: In Fig. 82B, use Chapter 5's alternating open-hand strum with your *i*, *m*, and *a* fingers for the sixteenth notes, and an *upstroke* from the thumb in the indicated spots. Tricky!)

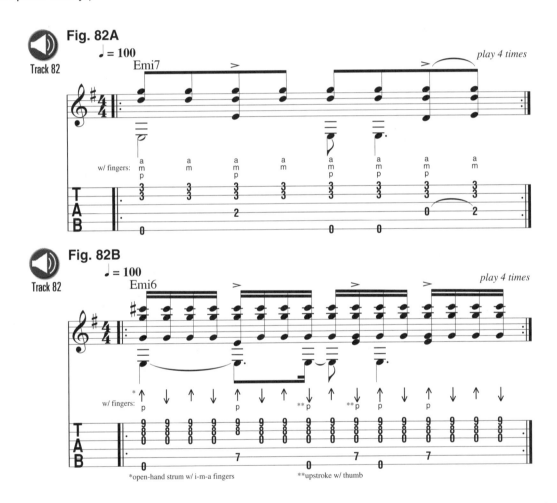

The preceding figures are merely highlighting rhythms that are played in a basic rock drumbeat, primarily to get you thinking like a drummer—a fun approach to try while composing your own fingerstyle figures! It's no coincidence that some of rock's greatest riff writers, from Edward Van Halen to Dave Grohl, played drums *before* they ever learned guitar. While we won't devote this entire chapter to mimicking drum-kit sounds, you'll find this section contains all sorts of interesting ways to coax "percussion" out of six strings, many of which accentuate the backbeat—rhythmic and repetitive moves you can use to get a groove going. (Note: For many of these figures, consider using the "heel down" or "heel planting" position illustrated in Chapter 5; you may find it yields more stability—and hence, accuracy—as well as overall comfort.)

Accentuating the Backbeat

Some rockers inject percussive effects into their fingerstyle chording with aggressive *replanting* (indicated with X's in notation and tab staves) of the thumb (*p*), index (*i*), middle (*m*), and ring (*a*) fingers, copping rock's ubiquitous *backbeat* (snare hits on beats 2 and 4). For this "replant" sound, you're basically putting your plucking fingers back in alignment to pluck again (i.e., the preparation posture this book has discussed in numerous spots); you're slamming them onto the strings just hard enough to create a percussive "smack." **Fig. 83**, modeled after Nuno Bettencourt's plucking in Extreme's "More Than Words," presents one application of this "backbeat/replant" sound.

Fig. 83

Track 83

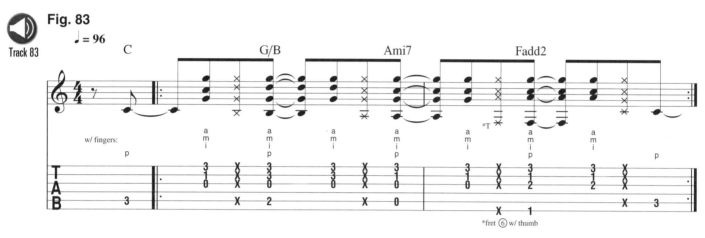

Backbeat Bonanza with Voicing Variations

In **Fig. 84A**, the "backbeat" effect is applied to fully fretted shapes, the percussiveness stemming from louder open-hand strums on beats 2 and 4. Note that each open-hand strum is followed by a combination of audible replants (again, notated with X's) and traditional plucking (*i–m–a*) of three-note chords. (For the quick exchange between these elements, try a "bouncing" movement with your plucking hand.) Also, notice how the thumbed bass notes on strings 5–6 mimic a kick drum. You can hear this sound in the work of pluckers like Ani DiFranco (achieved with open tunings) and several others cited within this chapter.

Fig. 84A

Track 84

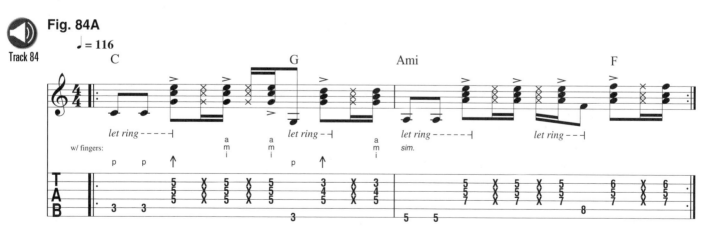

Fig. 84B is the exact plucking combination of the previous figure, only plugged into more interesting open voicings, not unlike those Dave Matthews uses in "Crash Into Me." Basically, these voicings (Cma7–G6–Asus2–E5/F) are the result of sustaining an E5 shape (E–B) over a C–G–A–F bass line.

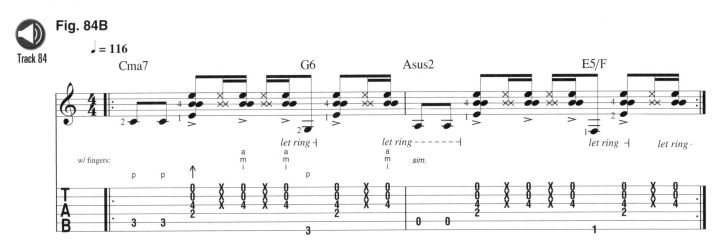

Fig. 84B

Track 84

Fig. 84C maintains this same percussive plucking pattern, only this time with voicings Jeff Buckley uses in songs like "Lover, You Should've Come Over"—three-note 6th- or 7th-chord shapes, played in conjunction with open strings. For instance, the actual fretted notes of this figure's Cma13 and Fma13#11 voicings are really just trimmed down C6 (C–E–G–A) and F6 (F–A–C–D) shapes, blended with the open E and B strings. Similarly, the G13 and Am9 chords are shell voicings (the root, 3rd, and 7th) of G7 and Am7, with higher open strings. As we studied in Chapter 7, these types of moves definitely evoke the vibe of an open tuning.

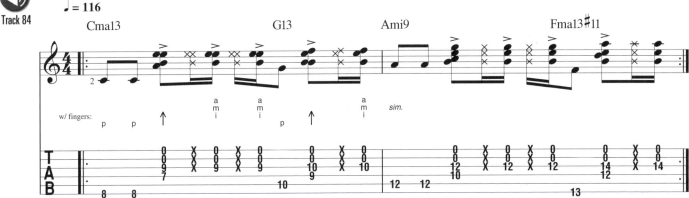

Fig. 84C

Track 84

Adding Chord Ornaments to Backbeat Plucking

In Chapter 6, we explored ornamentation of open chords in-depth. In **Fig. 85**, we'll apply these sorts of sounds to fully fretted shapes, adding suspended tones and pentatonic pitches to C, G, Ami, and F chords. Note the tricky plucking-hand moves throughout—open-hand strums and rapid alternation of the *p–i* fingers at select points. The end result is akin to Jimi Hendrix's famous moves in "Little Wing," "Bold as Love," and "Castles Made of Sand," as well as John Frusciante's riffing in certain Red Hot Chili Peppers songs.

Fig. 85

Track 85

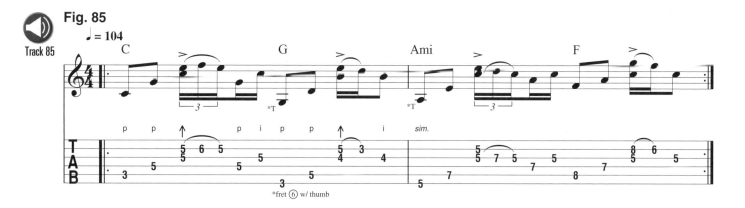

*fret ⑥ w/ thumb

Staccato Replanting and Choking Effects

Replanting moves can also be used to choke off chords immediately after they've been plucked; that is, instead of the *sound* of the replant creating percussiveness (like previous examples), it is *shortening the duration* of each chord, creating a staccato effect by leaving a pocket of air between it and the next plucked chord. When done repeatedly, and combined with accents at selected points, this creates groovy pulsations that are useful in moves like **Fig. 86A**. (Note fret-hand fingering recommendations adjacent to noteheads.)

Fig. 86A

Track 86

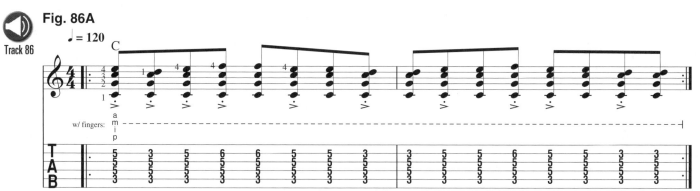

Fig. 86B puts this new technique to work through an Ami–F–C–G progression, with loads of added tones per bar, accumulating into an Ami11–Fma13#11–Cma9–G13sus4 harmony. This figure features a B–C–G–E–D–C melody, stated on the top two strings of each chord.

Fig. 86B

Track 86

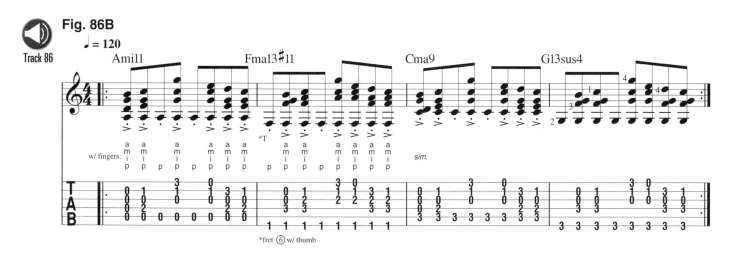

*fret ⑥ w/ thumb

Pull-and-Snap Technique

Your plucking fingers may also use a *pull-and-snap* technique for funky acoustic sounds, using the index (*i*) finger to pull and release strings so that they snap against the fretboard. In **Fig. 87**, a driving rock groove is established in measures 1–2 (a droning open-A bass note played in steady quarters, supporting double stops that are plucked on strings 3–4), followed by pulling and snapping of various A Dorian (A–B–C–D–E–F♯–G) pitches in the final measures. Here, nearly every pitch is pulled and released with the *i* finger; these are separated by percussive replants (X's), in preparation for the next pull/snap move. For the quick exchange between these elements, try a "bouncing" movement with your plucking hand.

Fig. 87

Track 87

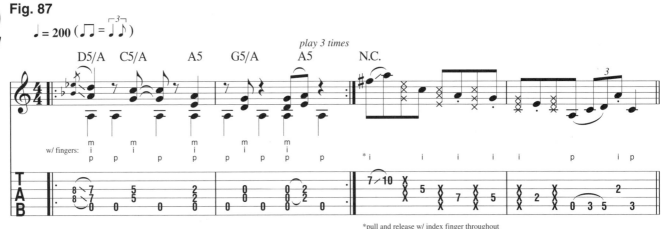

*pull and release w/ index finger throughout

Slapping and Popping Applied to Acoustic

Another percussive plucking approach, one not often studied by guitarists, is the use of a *slapping* and *popping* technique, a sound more associated with electric bass. Let's look at how this translates to acoustic.

Fig. 88A gets you off and running with a basic slap-and-pop exercise—a one-beat pattern repeated throughout a single measure. Here, each time *p* is indicated, *slap* the outside edge of your plucking-hand's thumb (at the knuckle) onto the sixth string via a quick flick of your wrist. (Tip: Try a *rest stroke*—slapping the side of your thumb *through* the sixth string, and then bringing its tip to rest on the fifth string. The sound may be more pronounced closer to the bridge, rather than directly over the soundhole.) This "slap" sounds the open E string; a quick hammer-on with your fret hand's first finger sounds the A note (fifth fret, sixth string) that follows. The hammered A note is punctuated with an index-finger "pop" on a higher A (seventh fret, fourth string), a move nearly identical to the pull-and-snap technique used earlier: Hook the fourth string with your plucking-hand's index finger and rapidly pull and release, forcing the string to snap back against the fretboard, sounding a percussive "pop." **Fig. 88B** puts these moves together into an F♯ minor pentatonic (F♯–A–B–C♯–E) acoustic riff. Bottoms up!

Fig. 88A   **Fig. 88B**

Track 88   Track 88

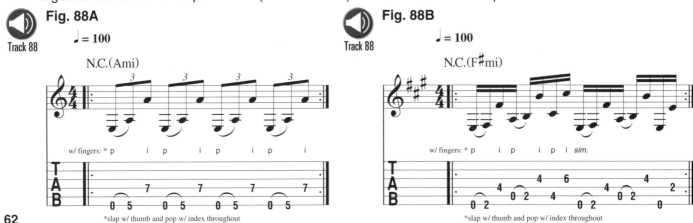

*slap w/ thumb and pop w/ index throughout   *slap w/ thumb and pop w/ index throughout

Fig. 89 presents slap-and-pop moves incorporating fretted notes exclusively, most of which are spaced a 10th interval apart, manipulating a C–G–Ami–F progression. Each measure begins with a chord's root and 3rd, separated by an octave, which creates the 10th. This note spacing is then applied to each chord's remaining tones further up the neck. This sound is somewhat inspired by the acoustic fingerstyle work on John Frusciante's solo debut, *Niandra La'Des*.

Fig. 89

Track 89

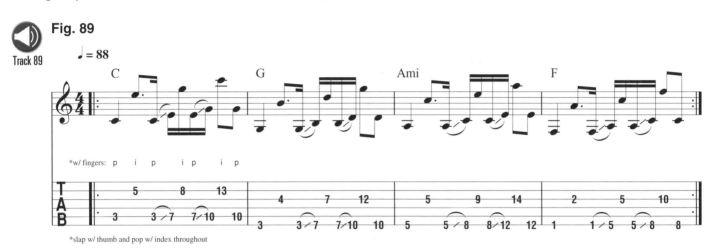

Adding Double Stops and Chord Partials to the Mix

Fig. 90 takes our foundational slap/pop and pull/snap moves and plugs them into a mellow, yet hip and groovy, combination of double stops, hammer-ons, replanting sounds (the Xs), and open-handed strums. In this figure, all of the notes are *lightly* pull-snapped with the *i* and/or *m* fingers, or slapped with the thumb (*p*), except for the Fma13 chord at the end of measure 1, which is plucked normally, and the open-handed strum (use *i–m*) of strings 1–2 at the end of measure 2. This passage is somewhat reminiscent of John Frusciante's fingerstyle riffing in the Chili Peppers' "Funky Monks" chorus.

Fig. 90

Track 90

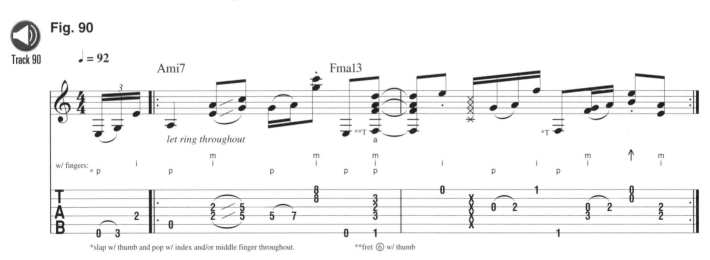

Fig. 91 is a more aggressive example of slap/pop and pull/snap sounds. It blends elements similar to those found in the previous figure, only plucked at a more intense tempo. Try a "bouncing" movement similar to Figs. 84A–C and Fig. 87 for the quick exchange between pull-snapped double stops and percussive replanting sounds (the X's).

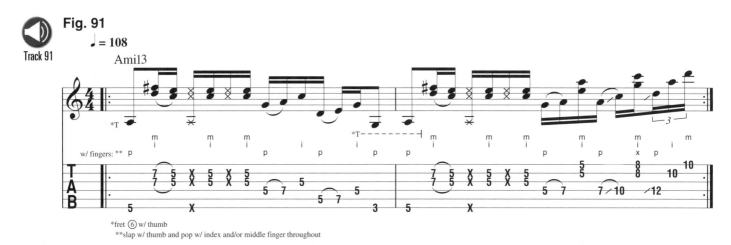

Hedges-Style Slapped Harmonics

Fig. 92 features *slapped harmonics* (notated as "S.H." between staves), whereby you're fretting select strings (in this case, strings 2–4), and then using your index finger to quickly "slap" across them at a higher point on the neck (e.g., twelfth, seventh, or fifth frets), stimulating harmonics. Since this figure's harmonics are all based on open strings, you need to slap your index finger *parallel* to the indicated frets to sound a harmonic on all three strings simultaneously. But make sure you don't hit the strings so hard that you physically fret the notes, like a tapping technique.

This approach is in the style of fingerstyle great Michael Hedges and the legion of pluckers he inspired. Use an open-hand strum on each open G–C/G move, plucking with your hand positioned *over the neck*, near harmonic "slap points," to ease transition between techniques.

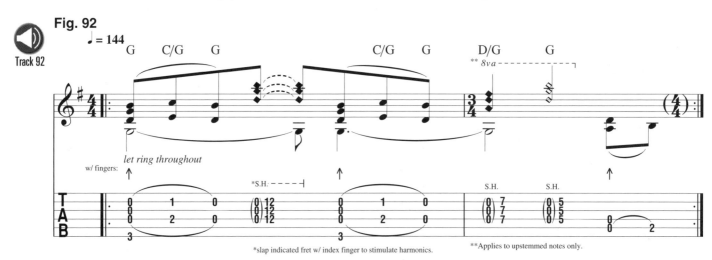

Tribute to Tuck Andress

Tuck Andress is most commonly associated with fingerstyle jazz, but his eclectic discography boasts much more than "jazz" tunes—he's arranged numerous cover versions of famous pop/rock/funk songs, from Michael Jackson to Jimi Hendrix! Plus, when he plucks his Gibson hollowbody on recordings, he records it direct and miked acoustically, which is close enough to fingerstyle acoustic-rock for this book!

Fig. 93 presents one of Andress' extreme fingerstyle techniques—a passage decorated with triplet double-stop flurries on beats 3–4. Try this with your plucking-hand's index and middle fingers positioned almost totally straight while fluttering them back and forth across strings 2–3. Then do yourself a favor— check out his instructional video, *Fingerstyle Mastery*, which is mandatory material for those who are interested in developing a host of other percussive plucking-hand techniques.

Fig. 93
Track 93

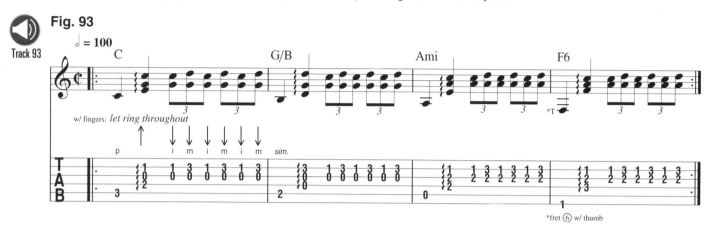

Tremoloed Bass Notes Using Hammered Roots

This chapter's final figure involves, oddly enough, hammered (then plucked) bass notes, played in conjunction with arpeggiated tones of C, Emi, Ami, and F chords. (You may find difficulty in fretting the Ami shape, unless your acoustic has a cutaway.) The end result, **Fig. 94**, sounds not unlike an *inverted tremolo*—the sound of a single bass note being reiterated as quickly as possible. Believe it or not, this is actually a percussive approach borrowed from Buckethead, who gleaned it from Parliament Funkadelic bassist Bootsy Collins.

Fig. 94
Track 94

Want to hear more percussive acoustic guitar sounds, beyond the artists cited in this chapter? Listen to genre-jumping "motherpluckers" like Tommy Emmanuel, Adrian Legg, Doyle Dykes, Preston Reed, Martin Simpson, Billy McLaughlin, Kaki King, and Phil Keaggy. Also, consider studying some flamenco moves like *rasgueado* and *tremolo*, as perfected by pluckers such as Paco de Lucía, Carlos Montoya, Laurindo Almeida, and others.

Pick-and-Fingers Technique
9

In this chapter, we'll discuss the benefits of *hybrid picking*—using both pick and fingers to achieve a fingerstyle effect. Many steel-string acoustic stylists use this approach as an alternative to traditional fingerstyle playing, minimizing the risk of shredding their fingernails. Other times, it's useful for simply creating harder attack sounds for driving acoustic riffs in which the bass needs to be extra powerful, or for playing very loud single notes that you don't want to "snap" (if plucked hard). Remember: A pick is plastic—a harder surface than nail or flesh—and when used with a swift wrist motion, can apply much greater force to a string than fingertips ever could. Plus, if you need to strum conventionally, play a funky riff, or whip out a single-note lead line midsong, the pick will already be there for you. Rockers like Edward Van Halen and Zakk Wylde, and multistylists like Steve Morse and Eric Johnson are only a few of the six-stringers out there who use this approach, both on acoustic *and* electric.

Pick and Fingers

Emi Hybrid-Picking Riff

Fig. 95 illustrates a heavy acoustic-rock riff sculpted from the pick-and-fingers approach, whereby a low open E is ground out beneath double stops, bends, and other open-position sounds. Notice that each double stop is plucked with the picking-hand's middle and ring fingers, while single notes are picked with downstrokes.

Fig. 95

Track 95

$\boldsymbol{\downarrow} = 76$

* ⊓ = downstroke w/ pick

Chapter 9

Dmi Hybrid-Picking Riff

Fig. 96 presents another open-position rock riff, this time revolving around a D5 chord and including many of the normal single-note moves you'd find in faster rock riffs, such as open-string hammer-ons and pull-offs.

Travis Picking with Pick and Fingers

We'll take hybrid picking in another direction with **Fig. 97**, applying it to a Travis-picking passage in the key of Ami, with numerous open-chord embellishments. For more hybrid-picking fun, go back and try Chapter 4's Travis-picking passages using pick and fingers exclusively.

Do you like the overall feel of hybrid picking? Go back to other sections in this book and rework some examples with this technique. All you need to do is think of the pick as a replacement for your plucking-hand's thumb, using your remaining digits (mostly middle and ring) to pluck the rest. In a pinch, the pinky can be utilized as well. You may even consider trying a *thumbpick* to achieve similar results. A thumbpick is affixed to your thumb, so there's no need to grip a pick with your index finger, leaving available your *i–m–a* fingers for "normal" fingerstyle playing.

Capo Usage

10

Everything in this book has been designed to diversify your plucking-hand's approaches, as well as hip you to all sorts of open-string voicings—two key elements in creating and performing various authentic-sounding rock parts on acoustic guitar. This chapter adds a little twist—a *capo* approach rockers use with open-string voicings to make their recordings and/or live shows sound more stereophonic, livelier, colorful, or just plain bigger.

For the curious, the word "capo" is short for *capotasto*, which means "principal fret" in Italian. It's used to shorten the vibrating lengths of a guitar's strings; when fitted across a fret (capos come in strap-on, screw-on, and clamp-on varieties), it stops the strings at that point, providing the player with a "new nut" and a new set of open strings, which are denoted by "0" in tablature). This makes it particularly easy to *transpose* (i.e., shift to a new key) a progression comprising open chords; simply move the identical shapes up the neck to the capo location. For example, this might be done to place a song's original chord voicings in a register that better suits a vocalist's range. Without the capo, barre chords would be the only other option—a comparatively duller sound on acoustic. This is an elementary capo approach; however, this chapter looks at capoing on a much deeper level.

Before you pluck through these figures, be sure to tune your guitar before and after you've capoed up, placing it behind and parallel to the fret, affixed just tight enough so that the strings don't buzz. Due to variations in a capo's squeeze/contact points, some strings may go sharp, however.

Capo Concepts and C–A–G–E–D

If you study transcriptions of some of your favorite modern-rock songs that feature an acoustic, you may notice that the song's main part is in standard tuning, while secondary acoustic parts might have a capo, used at a higher fret. This guitar plays the exact same chords but in a different register, maintaining that open-string sound via the capo. How do these people know where to put the capo? Let's take our ol' standby progression, C–G–Ami–F, and explore its capo options, using a specific process.

Fig. 98A depicts a hypothetical song's primary acoustic-plucking figure, played in open position and outlining a C–G–Ami–F progression. The remaining examples illustrate the *exact same sounding* progression, using *different* open-chord shapes at four other spots on the neck. To determine capo placement, simply locate all of the places where you can play the progression's first chord, C, using other major open shapes, C–A–G–E–D. To give you an idea of this process, next to Fig. 98A you'll see its first open chord transformed into a fully fretted shape at the twelfth fret. If you wanted to maintain open strings with that shape, you'd need to place a capo at the twelfth fret.

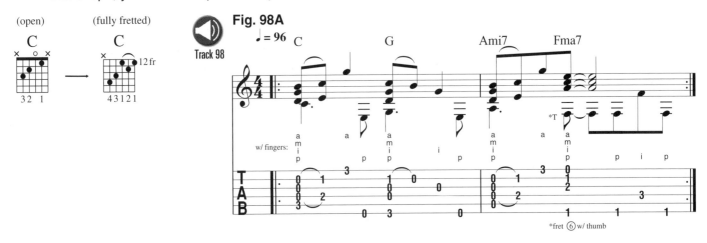

*fret ⑥ w/ thumb

Following this procedure, as you can see in **Fig. 98B**, playing an open-A shape with the capo at the third fret produces a C chord. A capo at fret 3 (hence Capo III) makes C–G–Ami–F playable with A, E, F#m (barre), and D chord forms. This figure looks and plays like it's in the guitar's "fingering key" of A major, but due to the capocd third fret, it actually *sounds* in the key of C, a minor 3rd higher (the distance of three frets).

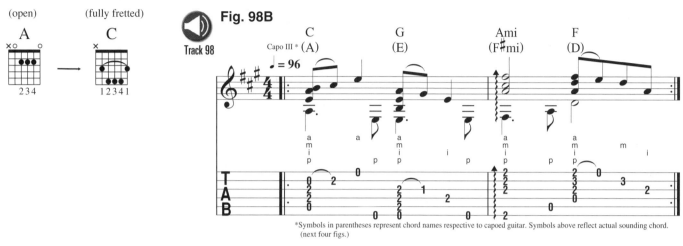

Fig. 98B Track 98

*Symbols in parentheses represent chord names respective to capoed guitar. Symbols above reflect actual sounding chord. (next four figs.)

Playing an open-G shape with a fifth-fret capo produces a C-chord sound. In **Fig. 98C**, Capo V makes C–G–Ami–F playable with G, D/F#, Emi, and C shapes featuring upper-register common tones. (The notated music sounds in C, a perfect 4th higher than written—the distance of five frets.)

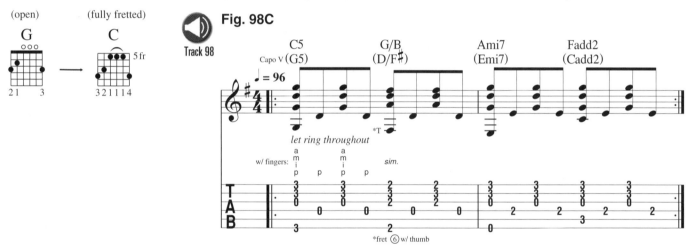

Fig. 98C Track 98

Fig. 98D follows suit. By using Capo VIII, an open-E shape with the capo at the eighth fret produces C, and the progression is now played with E, B, C#mi, and A shapes. (The music sounds in C, a minor 6th higher than written—the distance of eight frets.)

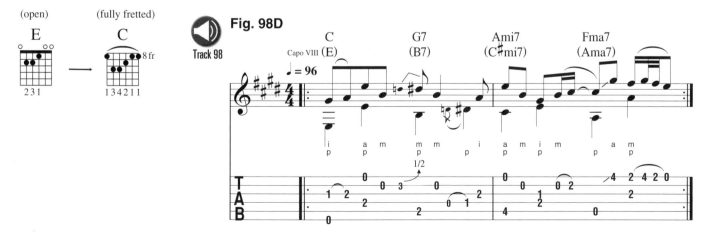

Fig. 98D Track 98

Meanwhile, our C–G–Ami–F progression can be played with Capo X (an open-D shape with the capo at the tenth fret produces C), provided you use the D, A, Bmi, and G chord forms of **Fig. 98E**. (The music sounds in C, a minor 7th higher than written—the distance of ten frets.)

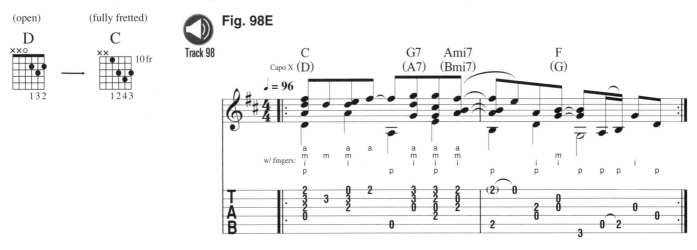

Fig. 98E
Track 98

Of course, this approach can be tried with other chords sounding the C–G–Ami–F progression as well: Find a place to put the capo so that Fig. 98A's G or F chords become playable using other open major shapes, or Ami can be played using open-Emi and/or open-Dmi shapes in different spots.

Extra Capo Concepts

Now that you've experienced moving the exact same progression around the fretboard while maintaining the "air" of open strings, to truly understand how this concept adds sparkle to a track, play Figs. 98A–E into a multitrack recorder, and then listen back to them in different pairs, hard-panning each. Or listen to them along with an electric guitar playing low-register, sustained shapes. Sooner or later, you'll find a capo's sparkling magic creeping into your own recordings.

Also, realize that a capo can be similarly used to maintain open-string jangle when playing in "flat" keys (F/Dmi, B♭/Gmi, E♭/Cmi, etc.), wherein most open strings do not fall in those keys' structure. Many piano-based songs are centered in flat keys. Use your capo to add a "new nut" to your guitar and, consequently, a new set of open strings; all you need to know is the song's original progression and, following this chapter's procedure, find a capo spot on the neck that makes it possible to play those same chords open.

This final capo concept is also useful for rock styles: If you find yourself playing an acoustic set, and your repertoire consists of songs played in standard tuning and different *slack tunings* (tuned down one whole step, down a half step, etc.), to avoid retuning between songs, start with your strings *detuned one whole step* (low to high: D–G–C–F–A–D). Then, for standard-tuning songs, simply place a capo at the second fret, which produces, low to high, E–A–D–G–B–E open-string pitches, and fret normally. Likewise, for songs tuned down a half step, use Capo I. However, don't get distracted by your neck's new "dot" positions!

Open-Chord Extras

11

As you've doubtlessly gleaned from reading, listening to, and practicing the figures in *Power Plucking*, there are numerous ways to vary the color, texture, and girth of almost any basic chord type. Looking back, many examples in this book depict different takes on a C–G–Ami–F progression, mutating it with colorful voicings such as Cadd2–Gadd2–Aadd2–Fadd2 and Cma7–G9–Am7–Fma9, and everything in between. To be able to spontaneously do this in your accompaniment, you need to have a fully stocked "folder" in your brain's filing cabinet from which to access heaps of chord types that may be used as replacements for stock chords. Access to these alternate voicings will enable you to experiment on the fly, plugging in a chord flavor that's appropriate for the style of rock you're playing. Towards this end, we'll close this book with a collection of alternate chord frames, all voiced in root position, beginning with a familiar "starting" chord (e.g., an open-position C chord) and following it up with fresh substitute voicings.

"There's No Money Past the Fifth Fret!"

This famous quote, a not-so-subtle reminder that the guitar is, in fact, an accompaniment instrument in most gigs, is often attributed to one of the most recorded guitarists in history, Tommy Tedesco. Taking a tip from Tommy, nearly all of the voicings that follow are played within your guitar's first five frets. While some of the voicings are considered "normal," many are not. You'll also encounter numerous open-position 7th-chord fingerings, spiced up into extended variations, with 9ths, 11ths, and 13ths added. While "barred" versions of these chords usually sound lame in rock, they *do* sound cool when played open, especially when arpeggiated or plucked with a percussive approach. (The "darker" sound of fully fretted 7th chords is primarily reserved for R&B, blues, and jazz.) Finally, with the exception of a couple sus4 chords, *all* voicings in this section contain at least one open string, which is key to jangle-rock acoustic sounds. Many chord frames also contain parenthetical notes, which are extra notes that may be added to suit your needs.

Realize that this collection of chords is by no means complete. That said, many of the fingerings presented here, with a little theoretical know-how, can easily be morphed into other types. To get you moving in that direction, we'll describe the "chord expansion" process in greater detail with a basic C chord.

1. Coloring Open Major Chords

This first section examines what happens when we take standard open major chords like C, D, E, F, G, and A, and get freaky with them. Each chord is played ten different ways in open position.

C Chord Counterparts

Many of the chords in this section will be colored in the same manner as the following C chord. By taking note of the tones added to and/or subtracted from C to create other sounds, you can experiment doing the same with other chords. (Note: If theory is new to you, when reading the following, think of the C major scale like this: C=1, D=2, E=3, F=4, G=5, A=6, B=7.)

The first two frames below, from left to right, take a C chord (C–E–G), remove its 3rd (E), and replace it with a "2" (D) to produce *Csus2* (C–D–G); replace it with a "4" (F) to produce *Csus4* (C–F–G). Adding a "2" or "4" to a full-fledged C chord yields *Cadd2* (C–D–E–G) or *Cadd4* (C–E–F–G), respectively. Adding a "6" (A) to a C chord produces C6, sometimes referred to as *Cadd6* (C–E–G–A), while squeezing a "2" (described in musician's vernacular as a "9" in this particular shape) in there as well creates C6/9 (C–D–E–G–A). Take a C chord and tack on a "7" (B) and you get *Cma7* (C–E–G–B); lower the B to B♭, creating a ♭7 (or "minor 7th") interval, forms C7 (C–E–G–B♭). Lastly, a 2 (D), 4 (F), or 6 (A) added to an existing 7th chord functions as a 9th, 11th, or 13th, respectively. The final frames add a "2" (D, functioning as a "9") to Cma7 and C7, producing Cma9 (C–E–G–B–D) and C9 (C–E–G–B♭–D), respectively. The highest numerical extension—9th, 11th, or 13th—replaces the "7" in these chords.

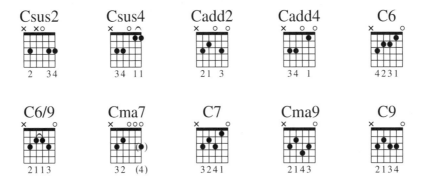

D Chord Decorating

These next D-derived (D–F♯–A) frames are mutated similarly: *Dsus2* (D–E–A), *Dsus4* (D–G–A), *Dadd2* (D–E–F♯–A), *Dadd4* (D–F♯–G–A), *D6/9* (D–E–F♯–A–B), *Dma7* (D–F♯–A–C♯), *D7* (D–F♯–A–C), *D7sus4* (D–G–A–C), *Dma9(no3rd)* (D–A–C♯–E), and *D9(no3rd)* (D–A–C–E). (Think of the D major scale as follows: D=1, E=2, F♯=3, G=4, A=5, B=6, C♯=7.)

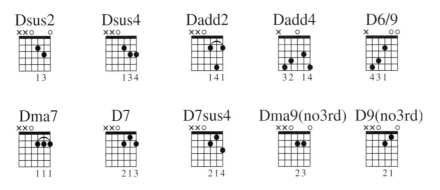

E Chord Extravaganza

Now let's watch an E chord (E–G♯–B) evolve: *Esus2* (E–F♯–B), *Esus4* (E–A–B), *Eadd2* (E–F♯–G♯–R), *F6* (E–G♯–B–C♯), *Ema7* (E–G♯–B–D♯), *E7* (E–G♯–B–D), *Ema9* (E–G♯–B–D♯–F♯), and *E9* (E–G♯–B–D–F♯). (Think of the E major scale as follows: E=1, F♯=2, G♯=3, A=4, B=5, C♯=6, D♯=7.)

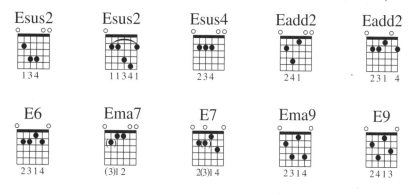

F Chord Freakout

Here, we fuss over a regular F chord (F–A–C), tweaking it as follows: *Fsus2* (F–G–C), *Fsus4* (F–B♭–C), *Fadd2* (F–G–A–C), *F6* (F–A–C–D), *Fma7* (F–A–C–E), *Fma9* (F–A–C–E–G), *Fma9(no3rd)* (F–C–E–G), and *F9* (F–A–C–E♭–G). (Think of the F major scale as follows: F=1, G=2, A=3, B♭=4, C=5, D=6, E=7.)

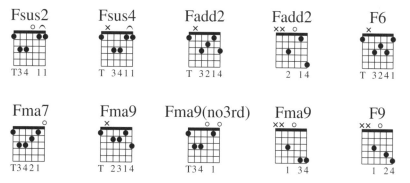

G Chord Genesis

Now let's go gonzo with G (G–B–D), creating gobs of related shapes: *Gsus2* (G–A–D), *Gsus4* (G–C–D), *Gadd2* (G–A–B–D), *Gadd4* (G–B–C–D), *Gma9* (G–B–D–F♯–A), *G9* (G–B–D–F–A), and *G13sus4* (G–C–D–F–E). (Think of the G major scale as follows: G=1, A=2, B=3, C=4, D=5, E=6, F♯=7.)

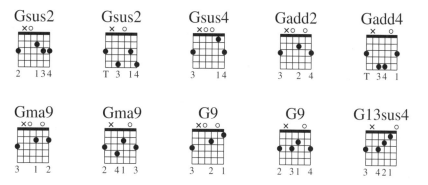

A Chord Associates

For this final handful of open major shapes, let's absorb some new A (A–C♯–E) forms: *Asus2* (A–B–E), *Asus4* (A–D–E), *Aadd2* (A–B–C♯–E), *A6/9* (A–B–C♯–E–F♯), *Ama7* (A–C♯–E–G♯), *A7* (A–C♯–E–G), *Ama9* (A–C♯–E–G♯–B), *A9* (A–C♯–E–G–B), and *G/A* (A–G–B–D). (Think of the A major scale as follows: A=1, B=2, C♯=3, D=4, E=5, F♯=6, G♯=7.)

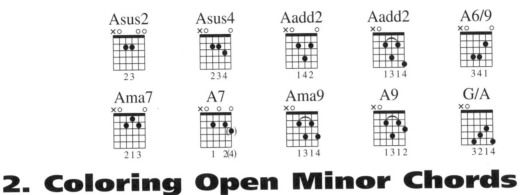

2. Coloring Open Minor Chords

This next section examines what happens when we take standard open minor chords like Emi, Ami, and Dmi, and elaborate upon them. Again, each chord is played ten different ways in open position. (Note: Although they're excluded, the *sus2* and *sus4* shapes from previous E, A, and D chord sections may also be used in minor keys.)

Emi Embellished

Now let's mix similar tones into Emi (E–G–B), for more evocative shapes: *Emi(add2)* (E–F♯–G–B), *Emi(add4)* (E–G–A–B), *Emi6* (E–G–B–C♯), *Emi7* (E–G–B–D), *Emi9* (E–G–B–D–F♯), and *Emi11* (E–G–B–D–A). (Think of the E minor scale as follows: E=1, F♯=2, G=♭3, A=4, B=5, C=♭6, D=♭7.)

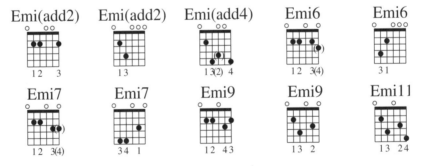

Ami Mutations

Adding certain tones to Ami (A–C–E) produces: *Ami(add2)* (A–B–C–E), *Ami(add4)* (A–C–D–E), *Ami6* (A–C–E–F♯), *Ami6/9* (A–B–C–E–F♯), *Ami7* (A–C–E–G), *Ami9* (A–C–E–G–B), *Ami11* (A–C–E–G–D), *Ami13* (A–C–E–G–F♯), and *Fma7♯11/A* (A–F–B–C–E). (Think of the A minor scale as follows: A=1, B=2, C=♭3, D=4, E=5, F=♭6, G=♭7.)

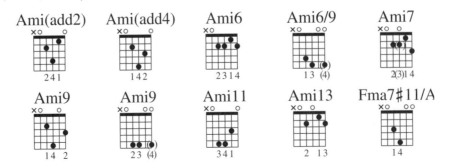

Dmi Developments

For our final minor shapes, we develop Dmi (D–F–A) into: *Dmi(add2)* (D–E–F–A), *Dmi(add2/4)* (D–E–F–G–A), *Dmi6* (D–F–A–B), *Dmi6/9* (D–E–F–A–B), *Dmi7* (D–F–A–C), *Dmi9* (D–F–A–C–E), *Dmi11* (D–F–A–C–G), and *Dmi13* (D–F–A–C–B). (Think of the D minor scale as follows: D=1, E=2, F=♭3, G=4, A=5, B♭=♭6, C=♭7.)

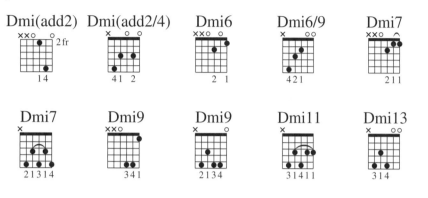

3. "Second Tier" Major and Minor Shapes

This section explores other "second tier" chords—fully fretted shapes like F♯, F♯m, B, and Bmi, commonly played in conjunction with the preceding open chords, only now adjusted to include open strings.

F♯ and F♯m Shapes with Open Strings

The next five frames depict different F♯ (F♯–A♯–C♯) chords—*F♯add4* (F♯–A♯–B–C♯), *F♯11* (F♯–A♯–C♯–E–B), and *E/F♯* (F♯–E–G♯–B)—and F♯mi (F♯–A–C♯) chords—*E/F♯* (F♯–E–G♯–B), *F♯mi(add2/4)* (F♯–G♯–A–B–C♯), and *F♯mi11* (F♯–A–C♯–E–B)—that incorporate one or both of the top two open strings (E and B).

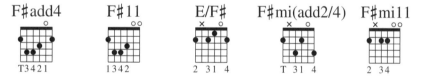

B and Bmi Shapes with Open Strings

Next, we have five frames that illustrate different B (B–D♯–F♯) chords—*Bsus4* (B–E–F♯), *Badd4* (B–D♯–E–F♯), and *B7* (B–D♯–F♯–A)—and Bmi (B–D–F♯) chords—*Bsus4* (B–E–F♯), *Bmi(add4)* (B–D–E–F♯), and *Bmi11* (B–D–F♯–A–E)—with one or both of the top open strings (E and B) added.

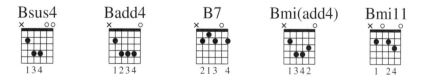

4. Open Chords with the ♯4 Added

When you're composing your own acoustic-plucking moves, you may wish to channel the mystical sounds of Jimmy Page's acoustic work with Led Zeppelin, much of which is the result of adding the ♯4 to certain open-chord shapes. These next five frames do just that: D5add♯4 (D–G♯–A), Csus2/add♯4 (C–D–F♯–G), Asus2/add♯4 (A–B–D♯–E), G5add♯4 (G–C♯–D), and E5add♯4 (E–A♯–B). Instant Zeppelin-esque exoticism!

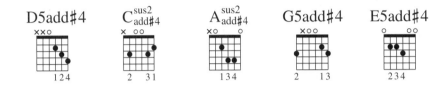

5. Oddball Open Chords

This final section presents fingerings for less common open major and minor chords and other shapes structured from uncommon root notes in rock/pop (e.g., E♭, B♭, F♯, A♭). These shapes are mostly the ones in this chapter that break our "within five frets" rule—but just barely! Once you work out their fingerings (they're all in third or fourth positions, with open strings added), you'll find these chords are easy to incorporate with other open-position shapes.

Cmi and Gmi Open Shapes

If you thought it was impossible to play Cmi (C–E♭–G) or Gmi (G–B♭–D) in open position, think again! Check out the possibilities with these five frames:

E♭ Major and F Minor Open Shapes

These next frames depict different ways to voice E♭ (E♭–G–B♭) and Fmi (F–A♭–C) chords with an open G string running right up the middle:

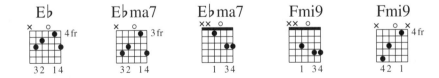

B♭ Major, A♭ Major, and G♯ Minor Open Shapes

Now we'll incorporate the open D and open G strings into different B♭ (B♭–D–F) and A♭ (A♭–C–E♭) sounds; the last frame features the open B string in a G♯m (G♯–B–D♯) chord:

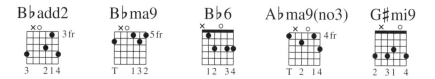

C♯ Minor/D♭ Major Open Shapes

Our final handful of frames addresses chords with a C♯ (or D♭) root, tossing the open E and B strings into the mix for variations on C♯m (C♯–E–G♯) and the open G for an exotic D♭ (D♭–F–A♭) voicing:

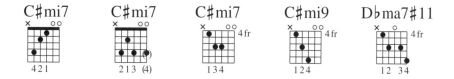

After you peruse this chapter on open-chord extras, put these chords to work in the ol' C–G–Ami–F progression (and others), grouping together those that share the same *note on top* (e.g., Cma7–Gsus4–A7sus4–F6/9)—the key ingredient for jangly modern-rock sounds! Once you've experimented in this fashion, go back and study the examples from earlier chapters, noting the numerous other versions of C, G, Ami, and F chords that crop up, many of which were purposely omitted from this chapter. Do the same with other shapes that were used in earlier chapters as well—Emi, E, Dmi, D, A, and so on. You'll be armed with an arsenal of awesome shapes in no time!

Closing Comments

Thanks so much for taking the time to read, practice, memorize, and apply the wealth of plucking examples in this book! I really hope it has helped you, the acoustic-guitar fingerstylist who *loves* all flavors of rock music, take your plucking to the next level, whether it be in accompanying yourself or others, or using some of these passages as inspiration for your own song ideas. Remember, pulverizing plucking technique and killer voicings are only a piece of the pie; you need to put these elements into a *song*—different progressions that are developed into individual sections (intro, verse, prechorus, chorus, bridge, outro, etc.) that flow in a fashion that takes a listener on a journey. Also, there is no substitute for studying how your favorite pluckers use different plucking approaches, progressions, voicings, and possibly even different rhythmic feels or meters (i.e., time signatures) along the way to generate memorable music, often within the context of a single song. I encourage you to *listen* to and *learn* as many songs as you can—the *entire* song—to truly "get" how the many devices in this book can be put to work. (Every chapter cites numerous songs that feature the techniques discussed.) This will give you a better idea of when it sounds best to play pianistic moves, use arpeggiation, get busy with bass lines, incorporate folky strumming, sprinkle in some chord ornaments, get groovy with percussive effects, and so on. The converse of this approach is also useful in helping to gain control over individual techniques: Grab one of your favorite band's songbooks, pick a song, follow the chord names over the staves, and force into the picture your own specific voicings and plucking approaches to experience their effect in a new context.

Lastly, to take your plucking chops even further, consider learning fingerstyle moves associated with the other acoustic styles this book purposely omits: new age, jazz, blues, country, Celtic, Latin, and, yes, classical! Most classical pieces demand that you control the sound of two or more distinct parts simultaneously—tons of tricky interplay between melody and bass lines. Also, try arranging a popular song (or piano piece) for solo acoustic fingerstyle guitar, capturing all of a song's melodic, harmonic, and rhythmic elements and adapting it for stand-alone performance on a six-string. Put any of the above ideas to work in your riff-writing and/or accompaniment and you'll be improving in areas you never dreamed!

Well, thanks again. I'd love to hear of your progress; any correspondence is welcomed and can be sent via www.intimateaudio.com.

Good luck and happy plucking!

Dale Turner

Guitar Notation Legend

Guitar Music can be notated three different ways: on a *musical staff*, in *tablature*, and in *rhythm slashes*.

RHYTHM SLASHES are written above the staff. Strum chords in the rhythm indicated. Use the chord diagrams found at the top of the first page of the transcription for the appropriate chord voicings. Round noteheads indicate single notes.

THE MUSICAL STAFF shows pitches and rhythms and is divided by bar lines into measures. Pitches are named after the first seven letters of the alphabet.

TABLATURE graphically represents the guitar fingerboard. Each horizontal line represents a string, and each number represents a fret.

HALF-STEP BEND: Strike the note and bend up 1/2 step.

WHOLE-STEP BEND: Strike the note and bend up one step.

GRACE NOTE BEND: Strike the note and immediately bend up as indicated.

SLIGHT (MICROTONE) BEND: Strike the note and bend up 1/4 step.

BEND AND RELEASE: Strike the note and bend up as indicated, then release back to the original note. Only the first note is struck.

PRE-BEND: Bend the note as indicated, then strike it.

VIBRATO: The string is vibrated by rapidly bending and releasing the note with the fretting hand.

WIDE VIBRATO: The pitch is varied to a greater degree by vibrating with the fretting hand.

HAMMER-ON: Strike the first (lower) note with one finger, then sound the higher note (on the same string) with another finger by fretting it without picking.

PULL-OFF: Place both fingers on the notes to be sounded. Strike the first note and without picking, pull the finger off to sound the second (lower) note.

LEGATO SLIDE: Strike the first note and then slide the same fret-hand finger up or down to the second note. The second note is not struck.

SHIFT SLIDE: Same as legato slide, except the second note is struck.

TRILL: Very rapidly alternate between the notes indicated by continuously hammering on and pulling off.

TAPPING: Hammer ("tap") the fret indicated with the pick-hand index or middle finger and pull off to the note fretted by the fret hand.

NATURAL HARMONIC: Strike the note while the fret-hand lightly touches the string directly over the fret indicated.

PINCH HARMONIC: The note is fretted normally and a harmonic is produced by adding the edge of the thumb or the tip of the index finger of the pick hand to the normal pick attack.

PICK SCRAPE: The edge of the pick is rubbed down (or up) the string, producing a scratchy sound.

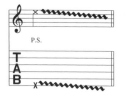

MUFFLED STRINGS: A percussive sound is produced by laying the fret hand across the string(s) without depressing, and striking them with the pick hand.

PALM MUTING: The note is partially muted by the pick hand lightly touching the string(s) just before the bridge.

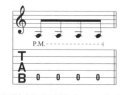

RAKE: Drag the pick across the strings indicated with a single motion.

TREMOLO PICKING: The note is picked as rapidly and continuously as possible.

VIBRATO BAR DIVE AND RETURN: The pitch of the note or chord is dropped a specified number of steps (in rhythm) then returned to the original pitch.

VIBRATO BAR SCOOP: Depress the bar just before striking the note, then quickly release the bar.

VIBRATO BAR DIP: Strike the note and then immediately drop a specified number of steps, then release back to the original pitch.

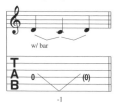

GUITAR PUBLICATIONS

Solid, contemporary teaching that covers it all! Musicians Institute Press is the official series of instructional publications from Southern California's renowned music school, Musicians Institute. These books, book/CD packages, videos and DVDs have been created by MI instructors, who are among the world's best and most experienced professional musicians. With in-depth, easy-to-follow instruction on a variety of topics, MI Press publications are designed to help guitarists, bassists, drummers, vocalists and keyboardists become better musicians.

The series:

- **Essential Concepts** – Designed from actual courses taught at MI!
- **Master Class** – Designed from MI's many unique master classes and workshops.
- **Private Lessons** – One-on-one instruction with MI teachers on a wide variety of performing and technical topics.

ADVANCED SCALE CONCEPTS AND LICKS FOR GUITAR

by Jean Marc Belkadi • Private Lessons
MI instructor Jean Marc Belkadi reveals the secrets to creating interesting, over-the-top phrases. This book is the complete resource for applying pentatonic, harmonic minor, melodic minor, whole tone, and diminished scales. The CD includes 99 full-band tracks.
_____00695298 Book/CD Pack $14.95

ADVANCED GUITAR SOLOING

by Daniel Gilbert & Beth Marlis
Essential Concepts
This follow-up to *Guitar Soloing* provides an advanced guide to mastering melodic improvisation. The CD includes 17 tracks for demonstration and play-along and the instruction covers more scales, modes, arpeggios, technique, and visualization exercises.
_____00695636 Book/CD Pack $19.95

BASIC BLUES GUITAR

by Steve Trovato • Private Lessons
Play rhythm guitar in the style of Stevie Ray Vaughan, B.B. King, Chuck Berry, T-Bone Walker, Albert King, Freddie Green, and many more! CD includes 40 full-demo tracks and the instruction covers all styles of blues and the essential chords, patterns and riffs.
_____00695180 Book/CD Pack $14.95

BLUES/ROCK SOLOING FOR GUITAR

by Robert Calva • Private Lessons
Covers: 10 complete solos in notes & tab; common scales and licks; blues, major, minor and combined tonalities; playing over changes; recommended listening; and more. Each musical example is demonstrated on CD, which also includes rhythm-only tracks.
_____00695680 Book/CD Pack $17.95

CHORD PROGRESSIONS FOR GUITAR

by Tom Kolb • Private Lessons
This is an easy-to-use guide to the most essential chords, rhythms and strumming patterns for a huge variety of musical styles: rock, blues, jazz, country, folk, R&B, soul, Latin jazz, fusion, ska, reggae and gospel! Each example is demonstrated on CD, backed by a rhythm section.
_____00695664 Book/CD Pack $14.95

CLASSICAL & FINGERSTYLE GUITAR TECHNIQUES

by David Oakes • Master Class
This book is for any guitarist who wants a grounding in the essentials of classical and fingerstyle technique. Topics include: arpeggios and scales, free stroke and rest stroke, P-i scale technique, three-to-a-string patterns, natural and artificial harmonics, tremolo and rasgueado, and more.
_____00695171 Book/CD Pack $14.95

CLASSICAL THEMES FOR ELECTRIC GUITAR

by Jean Marc Belkadi • Private Lessons
This book/CD pack contains 25 classical themes from the Renaissance to the Romantic Era and beyond. It includes works by J.S. Bach, Bartok, Beethoven, Brahms, Chopin, Dowland, Guiliani, Handel, Haydn, Mozart, Purcell, Satie, Stravinsky, Tchaikovsky.
_____00695806 Book/CD Pack $14.95

CONTEMPORARY ACOUSTIC GUITAR

by Eric Paschal and Steve Trovato • Master Class
The definitive source for playing acoustic guitar! The CD includes all 60 examples. Topics include: basic chords and rhythms; chord embellishments; fingerpicking patterns; blues, ragtime, new age, folk, and other styles; Drop D and other alternate tunings.
_____00695320 Book/CD Pack $16.95

CREATIVE CHORD SHAPES

by Jamie Findlay • Private Lessons
This book/CD pack lets guitarists explore the lush sounds of open-string chords. The CD includes 19 full-demo examples covering: arpeggiated progressions, arpeggiated chords and scalar lines, adding open strings to diatonic chords, and more.
_____00695172 Book/CD Pack $9.95

THE DIMINISHED SCALE FOR GUITAR

by Jean Marc Belkadi • Private Lessons
Learn the secrets of using the diminished scale in over 30 lessons and sample phrases. The CD includes over 30 tracks, and the topics covered include: tonal and modal usage; diminished triads, chromaticism, arpeggios, polytonalities, common licks and patterns for jazz, rock, and fusion guitar; and more!
_____00695227 Book/CD Pack $9.95

ESSENTIAL RHYTHM GUITAR

Patterns, Progressions & Techniques
for All Styles • by Steve Trovato • Private Lessons
This book/CD pack is based on the concept that there are a few basic, fundamental rhythm guitar techniques and a set of appropriate chords and chord voicings that determine the sound of each style. This lesson teaches the essentials for blues, rock, country, fingerstyle acoustic, Latin/Brazilian, jazz & swing, and funk.
_____00695181 Book/CD Pack $14.95

ETHNIC RHYTHMS FOR ELECTRIC GUITAR

by Jean Marc Belkadi • Private Lessons
This book takes you on a musical expedition around the world from Europe to Africa, South America, Asia, and the Middle East. You'll discover a variety of unusual and inspiring ethnic rhythms, riffs, and licks in this creative book and CD pack. The accompanying CD contains 81 demo tracks of all the music in the book.
_____00695873 Book/CD Pack $14.95

EXOTIC SCALES & LICKS FOR ELECTRIC GUITAR

by Jean Marc Belkadi • Private Lessons
Expand your lead lines and scalar vocabulary with this book, packed full of unusual scales and interesting ways to play them. Scales include: Prometheus, Hebrew, Hungarian Gypsy, Hindu, Neapolitan Major & Minor, East Indian, Romanian, double harmonic minor, Persian, 8-Tone Spanish, Byzantine, and more.
_____00695860 Book/CD Pack $14.95

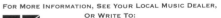